LIFTING THE VEIL
THE
FACE
TRU*of*TH

Also by the author

In Spirit and in Truth: 10 Bible Studies on Worship

Taking Note of Music

Sur le rock

Bibliographie d'ouvrages apologétique

Reasons of the Heart: Recovering Christian Persuasion

La carte protestante: L'apologétique protestante de langue française de 1815 à 1848

LIFTING THE VEIL

THE FACE OF TRUTH

WILLIAM EDGAR

P&R PUBLISHING

P.O. BOX 817 • PHILLIPSBURG • NEW JERSEY 08865-0817

© 2001 by William Edgar

Unless otherwise indicated, all Scripture quotations are from the HOLY BIBLE, NEW INTERNATIONAL VERSION®. NIV®. Copyright © 1973, 1978, 1984 by International Bible Society. Used by permission of Zondervan Publishing House. All rights reserved.

Italics in Scripture quotations indicate emphasis added.

Page design by Tobias Design
Typesetting by Michelle Feaster

Printed in the United States of America

Library of Congress Cataloging-in-Publication Data

Edgar, William, 1944–
    The face of truth : lifting the veil / William Edgar.
       p. cm.
    ISBN 0-87552-178-9 (pbk.)
    1. Apologetics. I. Title.

BT1103.E34 2001
239—dc21

                          00-066933

To Edith Schaeffer,

whose home led us to heaven

CONTENTS

INTRODUCTION

All people are bargain hunters. Not in the strict sense that we love deals or try to haggle for markdowns. But we prefer the relative comfort of spiritual complacency against the high cost of looking into the face of truth.

The styles of bargain hunters vary. Some are Faustian bargainers, waging earthly power and success over against their soul, which they must someday forfeit. The current quest for money and material security is a common form of bargaining in some societies. Elevating pleasures of all kinds, entertainment, and distractions—these are the least subtle avoidance tactics.

Many other tactics shield us from having to face ultimate questions. A person may claim to be anti-intellectual, pragmatic, and not interested in complex matters about eternal life and invisible realities. Delay is perhaps the most widespread bargaining tactic. Many young people, both in the West and outside the West, focus only on career and the temporal protection of a good income. People say they'll look seriously into spiritual issues one day or another, but later, always later. The fact that later may never come is not immediately apparent to the good bargainer.

Other forms of bargaining are more subtle. We can avoid facing the deepest issues of life out of fear. Sometimes it is precisely the fear that there may be a God, or the fear of his judgment, that ironically stiffens our inertia against seeking him. Sometimes it is a particular issue that keeps us from going further on any journey toward faith. A severe blow, something abusive, or living with tragedy—these can become obstacles to taking God seriously, especially one who is said to be merciful and kind. Or, again ironically, it may be religious certainty that keeps some people from the honest, free exploration of religion. The more legalistic forms may be the cause of closed-mindedness, but so may the looser, more mystical, even New Age, kinds of religiosity.

A powerful couplet in John Dryden's *The Hind and the Panther* says,

> For Truth has such a face and such a mien,
> As to be lov'd needs only to be seen.

The book before you is written in the hope that readers will see the face of truth, ultimate truth, and seeing it, will love it. The truth is in fact a person. Seeing the truth, then, is something like being introduced to a person. But not just any person.

There is a remarkable text in the Old Testament book of Jeremiah that says, "When you search for me, you will find me; if you seek me with all your heart, I will let you find me, says the LORD" (Jeremiah 29:13–14 NRSV). It is from the famous "Letter to the Exiles" in Jeremiah's prophecy. The letter is counterintuitive. The people of Israel have lost their land,

and all that went with it, especially the temple of the Lord God. Instead of teaching them bare survival in their strange new setting, Jeremiah tells captured Israel to build houses and settle, to plant gardens, to marry and have children.

For one thing, their exile would not be permanent. The Lord would return them to their homeland in 70 years, it goes on to say. And they would be gathered from all the nations where they had been banished. Judgment would descend on their captors.

But for another thing, it is always wise to seek God above all else, regardless of surroundings. Even when the captivity ended, the earthly security of the Jews was in no way permanent. They would never fully own their land again. The temple would be rebuilt and then destroyed, once and for all. They would be co-mingled with the Gentiles. More important than the land itself was the presence of God, which the Promised Land symbolized for a time. It was God himself they were to seek.

We are very much in the same situation today. We are the Jews and the Gentiles spread around the world. And we may wonder, *Where is God in all this? Should we not simply try to survive?*

No, just the opposite. It's a sure thing that if we search for him, if we seek him *with all our heart*, then the Lord will let us find him. But how will we know the way? What direction should the search take? Jeremiah's letter warns against listening to false prophets. In times of difficulty there are voices of all kinds telling us to go this way or that. Is there one voice worth heeding? Does God still speak to us in the world gone wrong? Does he speak in the sacred text he has inspired? If we look there, we will find not some abstract truth, but God himself, the object of all existence.

This little book is a guide in the search. It is a series of meditations on some of the problems facing anyone who is searching. Though it is not a book of succinct answers to the long list of objections to Christian faith, it does provide certain answers by getting first at the root of things. It stresses issues like meaning, forgiveness, and love. There is a challenge here to reconsider some of the tenacious assumptions we hold, and to give biblical faith a hearing. This book is intended primarily for people not yet convinced of the gospel of Christ. Of course believers may benefit from these thoughts as well.

There are so many ways to come to Christ, just as there are so many places to come from. It is impossible to design one text to fit every background. Some readers may find these meditations complex, overladen with cultural anecdotes. Some ought to pick up a copy of the Bible and work through the Gospels. But for those who have questions about spiritual matters and are ready to pass up the fatal Faustian bargains of our times, this book may help lift the veil.

ONE 🖋

IN THE
BEGINNING

Some questions are perennial. The question of origins is surely one of them. We don't ask it every day, perhaps, but it comes to visit us now and then, and often with great insistence. Where did we come from? Who are we?

WHAT ARE WE DOING HERE?

The room was full. At one end sat a panel of jurors. Facing them was a young man wearing a suit, it looked like for the first time. This was not a trial, though it felt like one. The event was the public defense of an academic thesis, held in a graduate school in France. The evaluation of a dissertation in most European universities is a rather more formal affair than elsewhere. People in town know about it and take it in, for an afternoon's entertainment.

In this case the subject was captivating, if somewhat abstruse: a theology of quantum mechanics. The relation of physics to metaphysics has of course been a subject of discourse from ancient times. It is brought into prominence from time to time when discoveries either challenge or intersect with divinity. A century ago, for example, Einstein's theory of relativity and Max Planck's quantum principle set off a new wave of discourse in theological circles.

Our young candidate had done some original thinking about how the idea of divine providence might be disputed by certain aspects of quantum theory. Following the usual protocol, he introduced his thesis, explaining his goals, the research problems encountered, and his conclusions.

Then, a surprise. Usually each juror (or panelist, as Americans call them) responds to the thesis with positive and negative comments, requiring the candidate to defend his arguments. None of them did. Instead all three of them focused their discussion on Genesis and evolutionary theory! The thesis was forgotten, at least till the end, when it did as a matter of fact receive approval. Nobody seemed to mind, except possibly the candidate. He might otherwise have been relieved except that he had worked hard at his thesis.

So why did no one care to interact with it? The young man's work had nothing to do with origins, or Genesis, nor was Darwin ever remotely in the purview. But that is precisely what preoccupied the jurors for at least two hours. The discussion was fascinating and in fact quite heated.

I pondered this for the next few days. Then it dawned on me. For most of us—even academic specialists—the craving to know about origins is far more insistent than subjects like theoretical physics. All that was needed to trigger the whole question of creation versus evolution was the allusion to science and theology in the thesis title. These brilliant jurors had been given the excuse they needed to address the universal question: Where do we come from?

And they were right to want to discuss it. It is a burning issue. It matters deeply where we come from and whether or not we were created. So much is at stake.

The question of origins is inseparable from a second question: To whom, if anyone, do we belong? Lovers of science fiction know that this question is the subtext of many films and novels in that genre. In the movie *Contact* Dr. Ellie Arroway's life project is the search for signals from extraterrestrial beings. Played by Jodie Foster, the young astronomer has been preoccupied since childhood with finding life outside the earth. She loved thinking about these things with her father, who, sadly, died while she was still young.

As a professional scientist she has managed to obtain government grants to set up powerful radio telescopes that might record evidence of intelligent life in the outer reaches of space. Eventually she does receive clear signals, which tell her how she can make contact. They dictate the details for the construction of a powerful traveling machine that would put the voyager in touch with them.

The machine is built. However, politics and ambition intrude, and a pretender tries to take credit and be the first deep-space pioneer. His scheme is foiled, and so Dr. Arroway goes, using the machine. She travels and lands on a distant shore, presumably on another planet, though it resembles a warm, womb-like heaven. And there, she meets her beloved father, Theodore Arroway, who explains different aspects of the life beyond.

The film is intriguingly ambiguous. There is some doubt about the genuineness of the voyage. An eccentric scientist helps her at crucial stages. Does she really go, or is it all in her mind? Should we believe, or be skeptical? Ellie Arroway is in fact an "unbeliever" about God's existence. She has a boyfriend who is a seminarian. He believes in God but also in Ellie. Belief and unbelief are pitted against each other, and viewers are left to draw their own conclusions.

The film is not Hollywood's greatest. But it boldly depicts certain themes thought by cynics to be banal or inappropriate in film, such as the mystery of the universe, the question of alien intelligence, and the existence of God. When it is decided that Dr. Arroway should take the strange journey, she is warned of the dangers. But she answers,

> For as long as I can remember, I've been searching for some reason why we're here—what are we doing here, who are we? If this is a chance to find out even just a little part of that answer, I think it's worth a human life, don't you?

The first three words of Genesis give a powerful answer for all times: *Bereshith bara elohim,* "in the beginning God created" (literally, "in the beginning created God"). Before the world was, God *is.* He created, and all things cohere in him. *Bereshith bara elohim* is the whole reason for the world, its present and its past meaning.

The universe as the Bible describes it is waiting to be discovered. But we don't need a machine revealed by aliens to get there. The truth of the way things are surrounds us. The universe speaks, not through radio telescopes, but through revelation. It's a speech so loud no one should miss it. Psalm 19 puts it this way:

> The heavens declare the glory of God;
>> the skies proclaim the work of his hands.
> Day after day they pour forth speech;
>> Night after night they display knowledge. *(verses 1–2)*

The psalm goes on to compare this revelation to the prob-ing light of the sun, which bathes everything in its radiance. Though neither audible nor verbal this revelatory speech is nevertheless knowledge, clearly perceived wisdom. The psalm continues,

> *There is no speech or language*
> *where their voice is not heard.*
> *Their voice goes out into all the earth,*
> *their words to the ends of the world. (verses 3–4)*

Various theories in medieval and Renaissance philosophy suggested there was music, inaudible music, coming from the heavenly bodies. It's a beautiful thought, but the mechanics of the revelation is not the point of the psalm. Rather, it is to say that reality is articulate, the purpose of the universe com-municates itself, whether or not we can measure its impact empirically. So how can we see God or sense the meaning of the universe merely from looking around?

Our inner perception is in tune with the external simply because of the way we have been made. The same God who created the heavens and the earth created discerning human beings. As intelligent beings, it is our nature to discern the meaning of the universe.

Everything reveals God. An artist once told me about an experience he had as he listened to the wind. Though invisi-ble, its power was unmistakable. He was painting in southern France where the mistral—a cold, wintry wind—blows down the Rhône Valley from the Alps. The ability of this wind to penetrate objects and people turned his mind to the divine Spirit. Invisible, yet unmistakably present, the Spirit can whisper or roar like the wind. My friend explained that when the wind blew it seemed to him that "it was 'godding' on the world." This is very difficult to articulate in a painting. He attempted it through suggestion, contrasting light and darkness, and using geometrical forms to render a closed object somehow open.

Paul Cézanne's paintings of the natural world are a dazzling allusion to the presence of God. Think of his still lifes. They are so eloquent he is credited with rescuing the genre from being merely an obligatory academic exercise. Think of his brilliant oranges and apples. Those displays of fruit became a way to combine naturalism, human appetite, and the mystery of nature's generosity, its harmony, its revelation of God's bounty.

The philosopher Merleau-Ponty once said that Cézanne could render "the vibration of appearances which is the cradle of things." His series the *Montagne Sainte Victoire* presents the enigmatic granite mass outside of Aix-en-Provence in every season, in every different light. There is no movement, and there are no people. In his technique he is both thoroughly classical, harking back to the Renaissance concept of symmetry, and wonderfully natural. The scenes are clearly paintings, works of art first of all, and our attention is drawn to them as compositions. Henri Matisse once said, "A Cézanne is a moment of the artist, while a Sisley [one of the impressionists] is a moment of nature." But then we also *see* nature in Cézanne, nature as it really is. As Jed Perl once put it, in his use of color and form he has a way of "rhapsodizing nature without sentimentalizing it." In short, Cézanne helps us to see God's beauty, but also his mystery, in the creation around.

Of course, God's revelation does not only come to us from what we call "nature"—the world undisturbed by people, buildings, and machines. His truth is equally present in the cities. One of my former colleagues, an urban sociologist, used to lament the pictures on greeting cards and church bulletins. They were always pleasant scenes of the out-of-doors, landscapes, animals, and flowers. These supposedly expressed the reassuring presence of the Creator God, an oasis from the difficulties of life. But, my friend went on, the cities tell it like it is. There is even a certain beauty in human constructions, buildings, automobiles, urban centers. These indeed tell us of life in community, creative architecture, mobility, revealing just as much about the living God as trees and hills.

SIGNALS FROM ALL OVER

God's truth surrounds us. It does come at us from the external world. But it is also manifest in us, in our beings. It is particularly present in our psyches. It has long been understood by savants that the conscience is an especially strong witness to the presence of God. We have knowledge. Though it is generated from outside, it is carried by our very selves, imprinted on the structure of our beings. My artist friend might have said, "It's 'godding' in me."

One of the most mysterious experiences we can have is reckoning with our self-consciousness. It may not happen very often, but from time to time, usually by surprise, we suddenly confront our selfness: I am aware that I am aware. At those times we may ask, *Why am I myself, and not another? How is it that I am aware of being myself, and that this awareness is somehow there for me, self-generated?* I can well remember sitting by the window in my parents' house on Long Island, gazing outdoors at the reeds in our back yard, as they swayed in the wind. All of a sudden, I began to wonder about why I was there, at that precise moment, looking at reeds waving in the wind. *Who am I? How do I know this is not a dream?* There is a certain mystery to perception.

Consciousness has a certain shape as well. We know, for instance, that we exist in some kind of time frame. This self of which I am aware is moving along in history. If I sleep, I will wake up as the same person, yet a day older. If I look back on the past, I can remember things, but never quite place myself back where I was. Most of all, I have a sense of destiny. I am going somewhere. Ecclesiastes, one of the darker books in the Bible, nevertheless reminds us that "[God] has also set eternity in the hearts of men" (Ecclesiastes 3:11). The allusions here to Genesis 1 are obvious. As God's image-bearers we feel the presence of destiny, the weight of time heavily upon our being.

Our basic sense of right and wrong is also a revelation of God. Contrary to claims that the conscience is arbitrary or socially conditioned, there are situations that make it clear we are dealing with absolutes.

Consider two persons having an argument. Let's say someone broke into the line at the post office and provoked the person behind. How will they argue? The one might say, "You can't barge in, I was here first." To which the other might reply, "Oh, but I was here earlier, and I'm just coming back to my original place in line." He will surely not say, "What does firstness have to do with the right to a place in the line?" They won't disagree on the standards (being there first), only on who is in accord with them (getting there first). They will share certain unspoken norms and then proceed to show who is right. Of course, one of them might call up a higher standard. For example, he might say, "I know you were first, but I am older than you, and you should let me pass." In some cultures, that situation could actually arise. But even then he is not asking for all rules to be dropped.

There are limits to this illustration, of course. But in ordinary experience, we often bank on assumptions that are practically universal when it comes to basic morality. Why is this so? Is it merely convention? If it is, how did it become conventional in the first place? Appealing to convention or tradition will not explain its universality. It had to arrive somehow. The answer is God's disclosure of the way things are.

One sociologist has called this moral sense a "signal of transcendence." This somewhat complex term means a clue, a *signal*, not a proof, that there is another realm, a world that transcends our ordinary horizon, one that is the source of these intimations from the conscience.

There are many examples of these signals of transcendence. One of them is play. Why do people enjoy games, whether in sports or in the parlor? For that matter, why do we enjoy *playing* musical instruments? What is it about the architecture of sound, the story of a melody, the sway of the rhythm, that appeals to us? Why do we laugh at a good joke? Is it not because we know, deep down, that there is another realm, one that is beyond the horizontal realm of ordinary experience, that transcends daily life? There is a realm where playing is the real thing, where laughter is always legitimate.

Another signal of transcendence is the sense of order. When a mother comforts her crying child, and says, in effect, "Everything's going to be all right," what is she communicating, at the deepest level? Strictly speaking, she really has no way of knowing that everything will be fine. Where do her words come from? Is it just a pragmatic way to quiet a child? She is indeed confronting the child with ways to cope with the world. But why not send an opposite message, one that makes crying only too appropriate? Because she knows, deep down, that there is justice, that the world is not absurd.

We know this because we are God's image-bearers, made to receive his revelation. To deny this is to deny everything we know, everything we are. *In the beginning, God.* The great question of the meaning of life is settled in those three Hebrew words: *Bereshith bara elohim. Elohim,* or *El,* the transcendent, Creator God, is the beginning and the end. But *elohim* has become one of us, so that there may be no doubt. Ellie Arroway's words, "I think it's worth a human life, don't you," are telling. God ultimately showed us who he is through Jesus Christ, who came to earth as a man, lived and died, and shone his light into our darkness. We are accountable for that knowledge.

> For he has set a day when he will judge the world with justice by the man he has appointed. He has given proof of this to all men by raising him from the dead. *(Acts 17:31)*

TWO ✌

THE REAL
WORLD

Can this God be known? How do we gain access to Elohim? What assurance do we have that we are not projecting a human need and calling it God? Perhaps no question in contemporary culture longs for an answer more than the question of knowledge. How can we know anything for certain? Most crucially, how can we know Elohim?

WAS BLIND BUT NOW I SEE

They say seeing is believing. A brief detour into the history of visual art is in order. Art is wisdom expressed through sensory media. When we look at a great painting, of course, we should not first be confronted with a philosophical statement or a moral. Moralistic art is usually pedestrian, like a bad sermon. Yet a great painting is more than a simple representation of a person or a scene from the natural world. One of the purposes of the visual arts, whether in the Western tradition or outside it, is to arbitrate between us and the world. A picture is a metaphor, a dialogue between the world and the self. Some painting is so close to the subject as to be photographic. Some is far more abstract, nonobjective. What matters is not so much the degree of objectivity as what is being articulated.

In Western art, few schools have the kind of popularity enjoyed by impressionism. Intriguingly, it was born in controversy. The term was coined by Louis Leroy in the satirical magazine, *Le Charivari*, where his article mocked the loose brushwork of some paintings he had beheld in a recent exhibit. That particular show has since become a landmark in art history. It had to be held outside the official galleries, in a photographer's showroom in Paris, in the year 1874. The paintings were done by a group of young artists with a distinctive approach. They had been meeting at the *Café Guerbois* in Paris to discuss new ideas on aesthetics, ideas that would greatly distance them from the official, academic art of the day. Leroy's criticism included disparaging remarks about "shoddy crafting."

One can understand the concern. There is something fleeting and dreamlike about some of the impressionist works. Indeed, the centerpiece of the show was Claude Monet's strange and powerful *Impression, Sunrise*, a hazy, pastel-colored, suggestive play on the light during the early hours of the day in the harbor at Le Havre. It's an astonishingly beautiful work: fresh, mysterious, captivating. It does give us wisdom about the water and the boats in the early dawn, a wisdom the academic literalist art could not produce.

Monet (1840–1926) once made the revealing statement that he wished he had been born blind so that he could gain his sight and thus paint objects without having known what they are. In other words, he did not want to be misled by any previous knowledge of the object. For example, when he would receive the impression of green, generated by a bush in the distance, he would not have to work from his knowledge of a bush, but just paint the light. He believed painting should reflect not the object itself but the light coming from that object to the eye.

There is precedent for this approach in the tradition of realism in French art. Jean-Baptiste Chardin (1699–1779), for example, gave to his subjects an amazing amount of sensual texture and weight. His themes are entirely ordinary: a silver goblet, a hunter's catch, a jar of olives. But there is magic in them. Diderot, the encyclopedist, compared Chardin's genre painting to philosophy. The good philosopher, like the good painter, is the master of the ordinary, not a strange genius. Monet, living a century and a half later, took the next step. He fell completely in love with color and light. The eye became an instrument to record them. Cézanne reportedly said of him, "He is only an eye, but what an eye!"

What lesson can we learn from the impressionists? To see, and not be made blind by convention. The way out is to trust the eye, regardless of where that may lead. Emancipation comes from trusting the senses. This move was a confirmation of what many people felt. The paintings were beautiful, free from the rigid artifice of the current academic style. They seemed to put the viewer in touch with something deeply appealing about the world outside. There was something liberating here, which gave greater depth and loveliness than had previously been possible in the art of painting.

There is a powerful analogy here to the knowledge of God. One cause of blindness to God is stereotyped notions about him. Different prejudices keep us from seeing him for what he is. So we need somehow to get beyond them. To do this, a sea change is needed, one that opens our eyes. When we come to this place, a beautiful world opens up, the real world of God's presence. The surprise is that when we do open our eyes we find the new world to be quite familiar. This is because at one level we actually already do know God. Though he is all around us, we have become blind to the most important spiritual truths about him. We need our eyes opened.

There is a telling incident in the New Testament that illustrates this dramatically. In John's gospel, chapter 9, a man blind from birth is brought to Jesus for healing. After making mud with his own saliva and rubbing it over the man's eyes, Jesus instructs the beggar to go and wash in a particular pool. The man does and receives his sight. He suddenly sees! Not only does the world around him become visible, but his perspective changes, he understands the way things really are. Not that he suddenly became enlightened or knew all truth. But now he had the viewpoint from which to make sense of it all.

This particular man was destitute. Both his background and his disability left him ostracized from the official religious establishment. When it was apparent that something extraordinary had happened to him, the religious leaders of the time, the Pharisees, questioned his claim not only to have been healed, but to have been healed by God's Son. They were arguing on grounds that look skewed to most of us but made sense from their point of view: given the blind man's background, he simply could not be trusted to report the events accurately. Based on his origins, he had to be ignorant. He was "steeped in sin at birth," was their put-down (John 9:34). Their argument was not so different from racial or class prejudice in any era. But for the Pharisees, the stakes were high. To have acknowledged his story would have made their house of cards tumble in a heap.

Presumably, of course, the formerly blind man did not know much about Pharisaical doctrine, though he would have known something about Pharisaical authority, as everyone did. It suddenly didn't matter very much! He had something far better than anything they stood for. He had incontrovertible evidence for his view: he had been blind, and now he could see! When interrogated by the paranoid religious elite, he gave answers issuing from his new clairvoyance. They asked him how Jesus, a man, could be from God. The answer from this simple, uneducated man was driven by a simple logic, reinforced by the incontrovertible experience of being healed: "He opened my eyes; ordinary men can't do that; so he must be from God." For which he was promptly ejected by his piqued interrogators.

This incident literally occurred. But at the deepest level it is a metaphor about opening the eyes. Ironically, those most qualified to know the truth, the religious leaders, had denied it, while the one least qualified had become privileged to it. Jesus himself disclosed the irony of the situation when he said, "For judgment I have come into this world, so that the blind will see and those who see will become blind" (John 9:39).

The bold step taken by the impressionists is something like the healing of the blind man. Eyes are opened to the way things are. Despite the reproach of the academy, the paintings make it clear that something wonderful has been discovered. They are fresh, direct, and alive with loveliness. Critiques about lack of craft or careless brush strokes seem hollow. One only need look at the paintings.

IS THERE A MESSAGE
IN THE MEDIUM?

The sequel to the story of the impressionists is also revealing, albeit negatively. From a commitment to questioning
the received tradition, the group moved to questioning
whether any idea could be trusted at all. They began to de-
velop a complete suspicion of *any* preconceived notion. Or, to
put it another way, they simply did not know for sure
whether there was anything real out there. The objective
world, if it existed, could not be known by the mind. We
must be content only to record the impressions received by
our eyes. It was a dramatic moment, one full of import for the
question of knowledge.

In 1888, inspired by the Japanese artist Hokusai, Monet
began to paint various series: fifteen views of a group of
haystacks, twenty variations on the façade of Rouen Cathedral, and, of course, scores of waterlilies. The subject was not
important. Only the play of light as received by the senses
mattered. The light and colors changed with the time of day
or the season. The cathedral was not painted as a religious
symbol but simply because of the purpose its walls could
serve the painter. It is perhaps the most secular view of a
church building ever to make it to a canvas! This is because,
as Monet put it, the subject is not a *view* but the act of *seeing
that view*. So much is the subject itself a mere vehicle, Monet
created his own garden so that he could study the effects of
the foliage. It was art about another work of art. Things became vague, misty, elusive. Reality was thinning out.

The big question arose, Is there anything out there at all?
If there is, can we ever know it? This was a revolution. Not
everyone followed. But at times the revolution became radi-

cal. Many years later Andy Warhol depicted a Brillo box or a soup can and blurred the boundaries altogether. What is reality, and what is art?

A lot was happening in this watershed period of history. From 1911 to 1921 the enigmatic Viennese philosopher Ludwig Wittgenstein (1889–1951) worked on an extraordinary text called the *Tractatus*. It would set the agenda henceforth for discussions about knowledge. He saw the world as no more than isolated "atomic facts." We use language as a way to assign labels to those things. But we have no way to prove there is any relation between words and objects. Words are like pictures, or models, which mirror reality but only from a distance. We cannot even know for sure what other people are thinking, let alone connect with the world around.

Wittgenstein famously compared everyone's mind to a box with a beetle in it. The rules of language forbid looking into anyone else's box. The only evidence for the beetle is that we have a box thought to have a beetle in it. But does it? Maybe the compartment is empty. If we are lucky, the tabernacle has a beetle, but we don't know what's really in our box, let alone in others'. Thus we don't know whether we have a hold on the true state of affairs, much less others' take on what is true.

In the ensuing decades almost everyone has been affected by the question of objective knowledge. No school of thought has been able to sidestep it.

This big question of objectivity is not only the province of artists and philosophers. It pervades popular culture as well. Consider the immensely popular television program in Great Britain (if not in North America), *Big Brother*. It belongs to the genre known as "voyeur television," seen in many countries and exemplified by MTV's *The Real World*.

The spectacle is based on a house in which ten ordinary people are fenced off. Every week they secretly present the names of someone they would like to see evicted. Viewers then vote to expel the less popular of two nominees. At last, someone survives and wins a large cash prize.

A strange incident occurred on the show. One of the players, Nicholas Bateman, was expelled because he actually cheated. He was caught campaigning so that his nominee for eviction would be voted on. In keeping with the realism of the show, his housemates confronted him, and he actually broke down in tears. Out he went. All this happened in front of the cameras. The event was reported all over the British news. There was even a class aspect to it, as Bateman came from a prep-school background, something many Britons resent.

Viewers of *Big Brother* sense that they have tuned in to something real. They feel in touch with people on the screen—like personal friends, or enemies. At the same time, housemates achieve near-celebrity status as performers. So, are they real people or characters in a staged setting? On the one hand, the cameras record every moment, which seems real enough. But on the other, how real is it to live in a house that is not a home but a television studio recording your every move, in Orwellian fashion, for millions of viewers? By blurring the line between ordinary life and performance, the show raises the question What is *real?*

The voyeur television genre is a parable for our times. It speaks of the great difficulty of moving from the self to the objectively real. Boundaries disappear in every direction. Consider the pastiche, sound-bite programming culture of MTV (Music Television). The famous chairman of the station once said, "What we've introduced with MTV is nonnarrative form. . . . We rely on *mood* and *emotion*. We make you feel a certain way as opposed to you walking away with any particular knowledge."[1]

In a way, television itself is the quintessential symbol of a culture caught in Wittgenstein's box. The lone soul sits in front of the tube and takes in the data, without a coherent story to tie the data together. Television has a unique capacity to present viewers with what otherwise would be quite incompatible images. Soap operas, news programs, music, films (old and new), advertisements for weight loss, basketball games—they all come through the same window. The viewer has only to press the remote to change from one universe to the next.

Much programming caters to a hunger for entertainment. Even serious programs are structured to hold viewers' attention. On many commercial networks even the evening news is peppered with advertisements. Newscasters utter the refrain "When we come back . . ." so that viewers won't switch channels during ads. The ads themselves are worlds away from the wars and elections featured on the news. Yet they become part of the same space on the tube. Buying breakfast cereal is somehow on the same level as negotiations about Palestinian sovereignty.

Again, the question is, What is *real*? Can there be objective truth? The screen, whether of television or the personal computer, has become a sort of mediator between the subjective and the objective. Through it the world outside enters our own. But we cannot be sure there is anything out there, anything besides the screen. In this kind of atmosphere, then, how do I know God is there? How can I be sure I am connecting with objective truth, and not the projection of my desires or the antithesis to my fears?

But wait. Must we doubt that there's a difference between reality and fantasy? Must we accept the fundamental presupposition of *Big Brother* as a given, the bias of complete skepticism? Is our uncertainty the only thing that is certain? Should the cultural drift that has left us wondering whether the beetle is truly in the box go unchallenged? Not for a moment. Though there is great pressure—even insistence—that we cannot know what is real, that seemingly bold inclination collapses under closer scrutiny.

This is not the place to mount a massive critique of the last two hundred years and the culture of veiled reality. But certain foundational issues do have to be mentioned. When someone once told G. K. Chesterton that his views were out of line with the twentieth century, he replied that the twentieth century was out of line with reality. In the same way, the present atmosphere of skepticism, far from growing out of an open-minded search for what is real, can be shown to have been based on a series of decisions—conscious or not—to *avoid* reality in one way or another.

Cultural commitments that veil reality are made incrementally. Monet's bold move to trust the eye was a choice. Revelation takes a back seat to observation. The positivists, contemporaries of Monet, proclaimed the death of theology and metaphysics, replacing them with the *positive*, facts verifiable through sensory experience. The real is what I can feel and measure.

Monet accepted that view, perhaps not intentionally, but implicitly. He once said, "I have always had a horror of theories. . . . I have only the merit of having painted directly from nature, trying to convey my impressions in the presence of the most fugitive effects. . . ."² Ironically, of course, his later paintings became rarefied, strange, reduced to the vibrations of light on various surfaces. In his desire to be born blind in order to later see objects as they are, he in fact made a choice to reject all objectivity. In favor of what? Here is the not-so-innocent part. In favor of an unfettered self. The strange consequence of this choice is seen in the later paintings, where the reality of the object seems to disappear altogether.

We find the same pattern in the general culture. At one extreme, New Age religiosity tends to celebrate the undefined energies of the world, on condition that all objective definitions be thrown out. But then how can anyone know even about energies if there is no way to define them?

In the moral arena, it seems that the only standard universally accepted is that of the right to choose. We are increasingly committed to a culture of choice. Only one problem. What happens when my chosen way becomes opposed to someone else's chosen way? Who wins? Small wonder that in this atmosphere we quite naturally gravitate toward narcissism. When the barriers to ultimate truth are so high, the barriers to self-aggrandizement are correspondingly low.

Let's face it. The rejection of objective truth was not come by altogether honestly. We have willingly become the victims of the veiling of reality. Why don't we see God? We were so bold to discount stodgy tradition. We've got certain things right. Our eyes were on the way to being opened. We saw many things. But finally, we could not see what was there. Our hearts wanted knowledge, but only if we could be autonomous, only if we could define reality according to reason alone, according to what we can measure empirically. We put selfish conditions on our access to spiritual truth, and ended as prisoners of the self. What is the way out? How can we find God?

We'll have to change the lens. Instead of looking at things through the culturally loaded lens of veiled reality, we'll need to try another viewpoint. Reality has not changed, but the way we perceive it has. With new spectacles we can see it the way it is.

It takes courage to challenge the deepest commitments of a culture that veils reality. That means being willing to look at our most cherished assumptions and put them into question. Here, though, we can be encouraged. God is patient to work with us, and willing to let us search, until we find him. We have been placed here on earth in order to seek God and find him. When the apostle Paul spoke, at their request, to the very diverse group gathered on Mars Hill, he described God the Creator at some length. He spoke of how God gave us life and breath and everything besides. He spoke about the way each person, each people group, has been assigned a certain place on this earth. Why?

> God did this so that [people] would seek him and perhaps reach out for him and find him, though he is not far from each one of us. For in him we live and move and have our being. (Acts 17:27–28)

The quest for God, then, is not an impossible task, doomed to failure because of the complexities of life and the veiled reality in which we live. We are meant to seek him and find him. That is why we exist. We already live and move in him, but we can actually discover him and know him. He is there to help us with the task.

Perhaps you are reading this little book because you have

come to a place in your life where you have decided to look seriously for God. Be encouraged that God is there to be discovered, and he will guide you in that process till you find him: "Ask and it will be given to you; seek and you shall find; knock and the door will be opened to you" (Matthew 7:7).

THREE ✐

LIFTING THE
VEIL

What needs to happen in order to find the truth? How do we acquire these new spectacles through which we may look at reality?

PARADIGM SHIFT

Surely, the first thing we need is a change of heart. Thomas Kuhn, whose *Structure of Scientific Revolutions* changed the way we think about the scientific method, introduced the term *paradigm shift* into contemporary parlance. A paradigm is a set of rules, often not consciously held, by which we solve problems. The rules change, not because we are necessarily drawn closer to objective reality, but because the new paradigm is more elegant, simpler, somehow more satisfying.

Consider the discovery of oxygen. Before the late eighteenth century most scientists held that the reason things burn is an ingredient known as "phlogiston." According to this view fire contains a hypothetical material substance, with weight and consistency, and when things burn, phlogiston is activated.

Today this idea is much maligned, but at the time it was a good theory, with excellent predictive value. Eventually, a number of problems confronted chemists who tried to identify this substance. For example, they increasingly noticed that there were different kinds of gasses and not just plain air. Phlogiston was an awkward idea, because these different gasses could be successfully identified without it. Yet the theory was resilient. It could be adjusted. When things burned, the die-hards theorized, it must have been from dephlogisticated air! Another problem was the strange fact that certain burning things gained weight, rather than losing it, as phlogiston theory said they should. Most of the time the phlogiston theory could be adjusted to accommodate such anomalies. Perhaps, it was averred, phlogiston itself gained weight when put into contact with various burning objects.

In the end, however, too many problems presented themselves. Though individually they did not require a radical change, their collective force drove a few scientists back to the drawing boards. In the 1770s, a new theory emerged, one that called into question the very existence of phlogiston.

This was actually no easy position to take, because phlogiston theory was tenacious. Though no single scientist can be credited, the French chemist Lavoisier was certainly the greatest pioneer of the new paradigm. In 1777, after years of wrestling with the issues, he proposed the *oxygen* theory of combustion. To get to this place, Lavoisier had to undergo a transformation of vision. It was nothing less than a shift in his worldview.

Thomas Kuhn compares such a shift to conversion. Because the idea of the paradigm-shift seems so subjective, Kuhn was subsequently faulted for relativism. That discussion proved long and involved. For our purposes, though, it's the fundamental idea that matters. What Kuhn surely got right was the recognition that in order to see things as they are, in order to know the truth, at least in the history of science, a revolution in one's worldview is often necessary. It is the same in the spiritual realm. Interestingly enough, though we don't know how far he went beyond science in his application, Kuhn was inspired for his theory by the story of the apostle Paul's conversion.

Told several times in the New Testament book of Acts, (see Acts 9:1–19; 22:1–21; 24:10–23), Saul's conversion to Christianity (and his subsequent name change to Paul) is noteworthy in a number of respects. He had been a religious leader, a rabbi highly educated in the principles of Judaism. But Saul could not accept the Christian account of the way Christ fulfilled the Old Testament. Indeed, believing that all of the history of redemption was at stake, he became a fierce persecutor of the fledgling church and did all he could to eradicate the followers of Jesus Christ.

He was on his way to Damascus with authorization from the high priest to drag Christians back to Jerusalem as prisoners. But just as he arrived at the outskirts of the city, a bright light from heaven shown down and overwhelmed him. As he fell to the ground, he heard the heavenly voice say, "Saul, Saul, why do you persecute me?"

Saul's reply is revealing: "Who are you, Lord?" He knew it was the Lord, because, steeped in the Old Testament, he could recognize a theophany, a special appearance of God to human beings. Moses had asked the same question at the theophany of the burning bush (Exodus 3:13). In effect Saul was asking, as had Moses, "By what divine name are you showing yourself, you who are the Lord God?" The answer came, "I am Jesus, whom you are persecuting." The name was that of the Son of God, the Second Person of the divine Trinity. He was the very person Saul could not believe in. Though Christians were the objects of his wrath, it was Jesus, their Lord, whom he was basically persecuting. Just as God had long before heard the cry of his people and would send Moses to lead them out of slavery (Exodus 3:7), so Jesus the second Moses (Hebrews 3:3) had delivered all believers and now stood with them in their afflictions.

At that moment, Saul underwent a paradigm shift. He saw the truth for the first time. Ironically, like the blind man in John 9, his vision was temporarily impaired so that he had to be led around by his colleagues. When he reached Damascus, he met Ananias, a Christian, who was at first understandably skeptical, knowing Saul's reputation. But the fellowship of Christ's followers accepted him and prayed for him. His eyes were opened, and he astonished them all by proclaiming the truth of the Christian view. He now argued with all of his acumen that Jesus was the fulfillment of the Old Testament, being the Lord's Messiah. When his former colleagues turned on him, his new friends enabled him to escape by lowering him in a basket through an opening in the wall.

Saul was renamed Paul. The persecutor had become the persecuted, and the opponent of Christ went on to be his most talented defender. It was a sound conversion, a shift in worldview, a *metanoia* (the New Testament word translated "repentance").

Surely not all conversions are so dramatic. It is a serious mistake to use this case as the only example. There are as many scenarios of legitimate conversion as there are individuals who have made the shift. But the point is that in order to know the truth, a change of paradigm is needed, one that makes a person open to God's revelation. The veil must be lifted.

AVERSION FOR THE TRUTH

Why is the veil there in the first place? It comes from a condition we all share, which the Bible most often calls *sin*. Not a term taken very seriously in contemporary culture. When we first hear the word, we tend to think of monks at their confession. We ought to try and give it another hearing, as it has a strong lineage as a diagnostic term. In its best usage, it poignantly describes what is wrong with the world. Sin has a primary and a secondary manifestation. At the primary level it means an insurgency against God. It is the opposite of the first and greatest commandment, to love God with heart and soul. It results in alienation and estrangement from heaven.

At the secondary level sin means refusing to accommodate other people as we should. It is the opposite of the second great commandment, to love our neighbor as ourselves. It is the reversal of all the virtues in 1 Corinthians 13—a favorite passage of so many—thus, impatience, unkindness, envy, resentment.

Sin can be active or passive, transgression or omission. The heart of it is being out of conformity to God's ways. It is far more than the failure to do certain good deeds. Its root is autonomy, trying to run our own lives without acknowledging the Creator. One of the most difficult notions to grasp is the gravity of sin. Not that we lack evidence. The human condition is plagued with evil, and when we allow ourselves to be fully impressed with the power of our estate, we can begin to sense the seriousness of it.

No better illustration of the true heart of sin could be found than the cross of Golgotha. When Jesus hung from the Roman gibbet, he was subjected to a physical torture rarely matched by human instruments of death. The victim literally suffocated over a ghoulish period of time. There Jesus suffered something, if possible, far more painful than physical torment. He was exposed and humiliated. The purpose of the Roman cross was literally to put you to shame in front of the jeering crowds gathered, perversely, to see you agonize. The innocent one, Jesus Christ, was thus treated as guilty and shameful, deserving of a death in public humiliation.

But Jesus suffered an even greater affliction. God the Father turned his face against him, sending him, as it were, to hell. That most intimate, most loving original relationship of the Father and the Son, which from all eternity was at the very heart of all that is, that holy communion, was ruptured. The great Judge of the universe had pronounced him guilty.

Why is this an illustration of sin? Jesus had not in fact sinned or done anything to deserve this fate. It is because he was taking the weight of sin on his own shoulders, becoming "sin for us" (2 Corinthians 5:21) as a substitute. What is sin like? Look at the blood, the torn flesh, the anguished spirit of Jesus. We don't often appreciate the evil of sin because we don't often gaze at it in its most vivid representation.

Sin is not a series of peccadilloes, things we wish we didn't do. So fundamental is the sinful human condition that theologians sometimes talk about "original sin." This means that sin did not begin in my life with a particular conscious act that is blameworthy. It is an ancient condition I have inherited along with my kindred in the human race. Among other things, it puts a spin of conspiracy onto the whole thing. In addition, it makes us attracted to ourselves and enslaves us to putting ourselves first in all that we do. We devise games by which we reinforce the condition.

Blaise Pascal, the incomparable seventeenth-century Augustinian apologist, expressed this social dimension of sin:

> *There are different degrees in this aversion for the truth; but we can say that it is in everyone to some degree, because it is inseparable from self-love. It is this false delicacy which makes those who have to rebuke others choose so many devious ways and qualifications to avoid offending them. They must minimize our shortcomings, pretend to excuse them, combine them with praise and expressions of affection and esteem. (Pensées, Fragment 743)*

In other words, we create a world for ourselves based on a lie. We then encourage others to reinforce our self-love by striking a bargain: we'll go easy on them if they'll go easy on us.

We do the same with God's truth. We will say the most complimentary things about religion so that it won't aim its guns at us. We'll claim a high view of the Bible and a vague trust in "the man upstairs," or extol the golden rule. These are so many ways to speak well of God in the hopes that he will speak well of us.

Sin is more than the sum total of our mistakes and faults. It is an *inclination*. It is something like having a sound body and then becoming extremely tired so that the body doesn't function properly. The condition is serious, deadly serious. More than being tired, we are asleep. And because of that we have no real hope for improvement. We need a radical change.

Can a change occur? Can the condition be cured? That same cross on which Jesus died is the answer for the ages. He who knew no sin became sin for us, "so that in him we might become the righteousness of God" (2 Corinthians 5:21). It is the great reversal. That death, followed by the mighty resurrection of Christ, was the sufficient atonement for all the sins of the world. Think of it. Whatever the guilt, whatever the infamy, all of it is absorbed and buried deep into the graveyard of eternal burial. It is the death of death. God has put away the evil, as far as East is from West.

> *Though your sins are like scarlet,*
> *they shall be white as snow;*
> *though they are red as crimson,*
> *they shall be like wool. (Isaiah 1:18)*

Perhaps you are in need of this forgiveness. Perhaps you sense the call of God to come to him for forgiveness, to be declared clean, white as snow. Whatever it is you may have done, whatever you may have thought, it can be forgiven. Some sin is prodigal, disapproved by society. Some sin is more inward. It comes from a cold heart. Quiet moralism is just as evil in the sight of God as overt transgression. But even the quieter sin of confidence in personal rectitude can be forgiven.

How then can you benefit from this atonement? Very simply, by lifting up the empty hands of faith. Ask for mercy and you will obtain it. Ask him to cause that paradigm shift in you, and he will. Do not under any circumstances try to come to him already changed. Don't improve in order to be acceptable. No amount of self-improvement will come close to what God requires. Just tell God you have blown it big time, and that you have nothing to recommend you. Cast yourself on his mercy, and as surely as Jesus died and was raised, so surely will God gladly forgive you.

Do you have a secret fear that you may have gone just a bit too far this time? That he can't possibly forgive this one? Well, he can, and he will. Look again at Jesus' agony. Was your sin covered by that? Was his death sufficient to expiate that? Of course it was. Faith is nothing less than acknowledging our blindness and asking God to open our eyes. It admits we know him, but we don't worship him. Faith is "a whole-souled movement of self-commitment"[1] to Christ as he is presented in the gospel.

Go ahead and trust Jesus Christ. You'll never be disappointed. You'll never be ashamed.

FOUR ❧

YOU ARE THE CHRIST

B ecoming a believer is, paradoxically, easy and hard at the same time. "Easy" because there are no preconditions to the love of God. We don't earn it; it's free. We receive it simply by faith. Yet "hard" because it asks everything of us, including a willingness to face opposition. The Savior directs our lives into afflictions that may be deeply unsettling. How can we be so emancipated and yet so imperiled?

A NAME CHANGE

There is extraordinary wisdom as well as piercing beauty in the old Negro spiritual "Changed My Name." It is usually sung in D minor, though it is modal, rather than strictly in Western harmony.

I told Jesus it would be all right, if he changed my name;
I told Jesus it would be all right, if he changed my name;
I told Jesus it would be all right, if he changed my name.

Jesus told me I would have to live humble, if he changed
  my name;
Jesus told me I would have to live humble, if he changed
  my name;
Jesus told me I would have to live humble, if he changed
  my name.

Jesus told me that the world would be 'gainst me, if he
  changed my name;
Jesus told me that the world would be 'gainst me, if he
  changed my name;
Jesus told me that the world would be 'gainst me, if he
  changed my name.

But I told Jesus it would be all right, if he changed my
  name;
But I told Jesus it would be all right, if he changed my
  name;
But I told Jesus it would be all right, if he changed my
  name.

On the word "changed," the traditional way to sing is melismatic, that is, embellishing the notes by bending them and improvising with *blue notes*, giving the cadence special intensity.

African-American slaves knew well the cost of discipleship. The price of becoming a believer in Jesus could be oppression (greater than the normal amount), chastisement, and even death. The spiritual was born in the clandestine church. Slave owners often resisted attempts to bring the gospel to their bondsmen because they feared it might confer a dignity on them not appropriate to their race. But the gospel did reach many slaves, thanks to courageous evangelists, both black and white. When they came to faith, they met secretly to encourage one another. They went out to the swamps and the forests, staggering their gatherings so as to avoid suspicion. And there they sang. They sang to their God, they sang about the life of Israel, they sang praises and lamentations. One former slave remembers:

> [My old plantation would] make the dense old woods, for miles around, reverberate with their wild notes. These notes were not always merry because they were wild. On the contrary, they were mostly of a plaintive cast, and told a tale of grief and sorrow. In the most boisterous outbursts of rapturous sentiment, there was ever a tinge of deep melancholy.[1]

The paradox of becoming a Christian is this. Lifting up the empty hands of faith brings two results. The first is *to be forgiven*. That is, we are "justified," made innocent. The second is *to follow Jesus*, who is the way, the truth, and the life. And so, on the one hand, we rest in the mercy of the Lord God; we know the truth that sets us free; we have had our eyes opened. But on the other hand, we enter the way of hardship. The step of faith is not simply a new preference or even a change of convictions. It is more even than a paradigm shift, helpful as this concept can be in understanding conversion. The step of faith is a new allegiance. Peace and joy are not the only features of the new alliance. There is also adversity, suffering, sorrow, because we belong to Jesus.

The spiritual has it right. If you ask Jesus to change your name, you are taking a step of faith. You agree, more than that, you *believe* he should come into your life. You have spoken to Jesus, *told* him it's all right. When you hold this conversation with him, he does change you. But now something matters more than your own agenda, your own set of values, your own security. Jesus won't violate who you are, but he may send you on a path of difficulty and opposition, just as he did to Saul when he became the apostle Paul. So he warns you: you will have to "live humble," and the world will be against you.

Think about it. There is a price to pay. It is not that you pay for redemption. That is accomplished once and for all by Jesus Christ. But there is a cost to belonging to Jesus Christ. This is because Jesus himself suffers with his people, even now. And so we consequently suffer with him, until the day when we are fully released from all bondage.

When C. S. Lewis became a believer, after a long struggle with spiritual issues, he called himself "the most reluctant convert in all England." Why? Presumably because he had begun to measure the cost. And in fact he was kept from holding a chair at Oxford, a position he more than deserved. His Christian faith made him an embarrassment to academe.

The spiritual goes on to reiterate, "*But, I told Jesus it would be all right. . . .*" Counting the cost is important. But it should never be a final obstacle to faith, for God can over-come whatever cost is involved. Indeed, he honors believers by allowing them the privilege of suffering for him, through which they discover the depth of his comfort and become whole.

COSTLY TRUTH

Pontius Pilate has been portrayed variously as a puppet, a shrewd politician, and a coward. Whatever else he was, he was a Roman governor who had to answer to Rome. His as-signed portion of the empire was not an easy one. There was perpetual unrest. Different revolutionaries and zealots traveled around stirring up trouble. And the Jewish establishment—living in an occupied land under duress—believed that God would overthrow the Romans one day and restore their sovereignty.

The Jews in Palestine lived by a political arrangement whereby they were given certain freedoms in exchange for their allegiance. The high court, the Sanhedrin, was granted certain powers over its subjects, though it could not exercise the death penalty. For that they had to bring the case to Pilate, who was not always amenable. Not only was he not particularly interested in the fine points of Jewish law, but he feared for his job. He could be ruthless, as was evidenced when he took from the sacred treasury to build an aqueduct in Jerusalem. In the resistance that followed, he ordered troops to massacre hundreds of Jews. Or, he could seem accommodating, tolerant, letting the Sanhedrin exceed its authority. One can get a certain sense of the dynamics of this culture by reading the story of *Ben Hur*, or watching the classic film.

Early in the morning of Good Friday, the Sanhedrin brought Jesus to Pilate in the hopes they could persuade him to put him to death (see John 18:28–19:20). When Pilate showed a lack of interest—not to say disdain for their case—they altered the charge to treason against Rome. Pilate was of two minds. He feared for his job. His reputation with Rome was already under scrutiny, because he had mishandled some of the conflicts he inherited. Failure in leadership represented the loss of identity for a Roman proconsul. At the same time, Pilate knew the Sanhedrin's charge was unlikely. From what he could gather about Jesus, any seditious views he might have held were other-worldly.

Pilate was unsettled by the accused prisoner. Jesus seemed calm, in control. He explained that his kingdom was "not of this world" (John 18:36). This may have astonished the governor, who lived in a Roman universe of battles, laws, risks, and this-worldly commitments. But still, he was intrigued. He noticeably wanted to give Jesus the benefit of the doubt. But at one point, a decision had to be made. A pronouncement had to be handed down.

Pilate addressed Jesus point blank, "You are a king, then!" Jesus answered, "You are right in saying I am a king." Then he added these words: "In fact, for this reason I was born, and for this I came into the world, to testify to the truth. . . ." And then, Pilate's fateful words: "What is truth?" (John 18:37–38).

What was the governor asking about? Perhaps he had studied the Greek and Roman philosophers and poets, yet could not find the answer. He may have read the Stoics and Epicureans without satisfaction. Perhaps he belonged to a secret cult, such as Mithraism, but found no lasting meaning and values there. What is truth? Pilate may have gazed at the great statuary and architecture in the cities and, though impressed, come up empty on art as the purveyor of truth. Surely the discipline and fairness of the Roman legal system had touched his pride, but would it last? Was it not fragile, subject to vanity underneath it all?

Was the truth then to be found in Judaism? He knew a fair amount about this local religion. There was much to commend it. Still, in which part, from which prophet could the truth be found? There were so many. Besides, Pilate had grown doubtful of anything good coming from a religion that claimed to have the oracles of God but then used its theology to such political ends. Perhaps, as would be true of Michel

Foucault centuries later, Pilate suspected that all ideas were masks for power, and so he was resigned to the absence of objective answers to the issues of life.

Indeed, there was resignation in his tone. The flame of genuine inquiry burned very dim. He was all too eager to resolve this case and have done with it.

The tragic irony is that the truth stood right in front of him. Jesus Christ not only came into the world to testify of the truth, as he told Pilate—he was the truth. The extraordinary prologue to John's gospel tells us that Jesus is the Word. He is *logos*, the revelation from God, the Old Testament come to fulfillment. He is the Word made flesh. He is glorious and came from the Father, full of grace and truth (John 1:14). This is why the apostle Paul and all the genuine prophets of the first century would preach the "word of truth, the gospel." This good news was received by believers and produced fruit in them ever since "the day [they had] heard it and understood God's grace in all its truth" (Colossians 1:6).

Pilate tried several tactics to resolve this case without acceding to the Sanhedrin's demands. He sent Jesus to his rival, Herod Antipas, tetrarch of Galilee, for interrogation. But Herod only mocked Jesus, tortured him, and sent him back. Pilate offered the crowds to release Jesus according to the yearly custom whereby pardon was offered to an offender. But they chose the release of a violent zealot named Barabbas instead. Even Pilate's wife, Claudia, urged him not to go through with this. He asked the crowd why he should condemn Jesus. But in the end, Pilate gave in. He washed his hands, and surrendered Jesus to them as if he were not responsible. *Ecce homo*, "Behold, the man," he yelled out as he presented the innocent Christ to his henchmen.

Jesus was crucified, died, and was buried. In his death he took on his bloody shoulders the guilt, and then the sentence, for the evils of others. That was Friday evening. On Saturday, all had been accomplished, and he rested in the peace of the Father. Sunday morning he rose again from the grave, alive and well. He had triumphed over evil and indeed had overcome the world. This victory was the end of ordinary history and the beginning of the new world order. It was like D-Day, the turning point of the war. While the war goes on a bit longer, the crucial battle has been won, and the end already inaugurated.

Pilate never saw it. Many of the Jews never saw it. "Yet to all who received him, to those who believed in his name, he gave the right to become children of God" (John 1:12). Forgiveness through sacrifice had always been the way to God. This is the one great lesson of the many threads that weave into the Old Testament. But now, all things are accomplished. And the good news of justification—God's acquittal for our evils—is offered to all who would lift up the empty hands of faith. The warrant for coming to him in faith is not that you may be religious. It is not that you are somehow chosen by God, which, of course, you cannot know until you are reconciled to him. The warrant is,

> the fact that Christ, in the glory of his person, in the perfection of his finished work, and in the efficacy of his exalted activity as King and Savior, is presented to us in the full, free, and unrestricted overture of the gospel.[2]

The warrant for faith is nothing less than the mercy of God in Jesus Christ. He promises grace to anyone who would come and ask him to "change my name."

This is not a leap of faith. Nor is it to "get religion." There is almost nothing in common between becoming a Christian and delving into spirituality. So it is critical that we be clear about this Christ in whom the treasure of grace is found.

When Jesus asked his disciples who they thought he was, they reported what people were saying about him. Some said he was John the Baptist. It was true that John had come to exercise a powerful ministry and that he had made quite a mark on the local society. Others said Jesus was Elijah. This strange notion was understandable. The last book in the Old Testament had predicted that Elijah would return before the great Day of the Lord (Malachi 4:5–6). Jesus had to explain to the disciples that this prediction in fact referred to John the Baptist, who did exactly what it said he would: prepare his audience for the judgment. Except the judgment would first be meted out on Jesus, judged on our behalf. So Jesus pressed the question about his identity by asking the disciples not for reports from the crowds, but for their own view. Peter answered, "You are the Christ [the Messiah], the Son of the living God" (Matthew 16:13–16).

Peter—often the rash enthusiast who could put his foot in his mouth faster than the others—this time had got it right. The Old Testament had predicted over and over that God would send an anointed one to carry out his purposes. What would God's purpose be? To establish a kingdom, one characterized by both righteousness and right worship. The prophet Daniel had spoken of "one like a son of man, coming with the clouds of heaven." He would be given authority and power over all peoples (Daniel 7:13–14).

YOU ARE THE CHRIST 47

The disciples would see him in a cloud at the mount of Transfiguration—where they also saw Moses and Elijah—speaking of his impending voyage to Jerusalem (Luke 9:29–36). Yet also, something they were less apt to accept right away, the anointed one would also be a suffering servant, one who would "take up our infirmities and carry our sorrows . . . stricken by God . . . pierced for our transgressions" (Isaiah 53:4–5). The true Messiah would be both humiliated and exalted, afflicted and vindicated. All authority would be given to him both to save and to judge. Peter may not have understood all of this. He even balked at the idea of Jesus being crucified. But he did recognize in Jesus all of those promises from the Scriptures about the nature of God's anointed one.

So this was the Messiah. As God's Son, he was part of the divine Trinity. We know it from the data of Scripture. We probably have a better perspective on it than Peter did. God is one God, yet in three persons. There is great mystery here. But suffice it to say, the Father, the Son, and the Holy Spirit are three centers of consciousness, three equal persons, yet somehow one God. God is one; God is three. Contrary to what various medieval theologians posited, there is no hidden *essence* of God "behind" the persons. God is one person. God is three persons! Three-in-one, or one-in-three.

The God revealed in redemptive history, the God made known on the pages of the Bible, is utterly unique. Unlike Allah, the God of Islam, he is three persons. Christ, the Son of God is no mere human prophet, as Muslims believe. He is God, who became flesh by adding humanity to himself: one person, two natures. Unlike the gods of Hinduism, he is one God. He does not have parts, nor is he divided. The three persons are not division or aspects. They are . . . God!

Furthermore, if God is not the Trinity, then we do not have an adequate basis for our faith. He cannot accomplish redemption. Why?

Consider, first, that the Son abdicated his divine status in order to become a man. He did not, of course, give up his divinity. But he gave up his heavenly glory to become a man. It was as a man that he could serve humanity. It was as a man that he could weep, suffer, and die. It was as a man that he could burst out of the grave.

Consider, second, that he did this all under the authority of God the Father. There was a divine agreement between Father and Son. The Son gladly directed his life according to his Father's will. His suffering and death were the necessary consequence of carrying the guilt of the world on his shoulders. Paradoxically, it was the Father who condemned him, the Father who abandoned him, so that he would cry out from the cross, "My God, my God, why have you forsaken me?" But it was also the Father who loved him more than anything, who kept his hand on him, and rewarded his obedient suffering with resounding victory. It was the Father who would raise him from the dead.

The account is not complete without the work of the third person, the Holy Spirit. He is the Spirit of Christ. This equally divine member of the Holy Trinity caused the incarnation of the Son, who was, as the creed says, "conceived by the Holy Spirit, born of the Virgin Mary." The Spirit of God gave definition to the Messiah. He was the anointed one, anointed with the Holy Spirit. That same Spirit led Jesus throughout his entire ministry. He is also the Spirit of the Father. The Spirit was the Father's agent in the resurrection, and now lives in the believer to give him new life.

And if the Spirit of him who raised Jesus from the dead is living in you, he who raised Christ from the dead will also give life to your mortal bodies through his Spirit, who lives in you. (Romans 8:11)

So, without the Spirit, there would be no application of re-demptive virtues, no animation in the life of the believer, in short, no salvation. Furthermore, the Holy Spirit character-izes the age of the kingdom, and brings the entire cosmos to full consummation.

Believing in the gospel, with the concomitant sea change this trust implies, is no leap of faith. It is the knowledge of God as Father, Son, and Holy Spirit that is revealed in the gospel. It is the understanding that because of Christ's death and resurrection, the eradication of guilt and the victory over evil are not mere possibilities, but firm facts. It is the clear perception that we are without any humanly grounded hope, but that because of the cooperation of the three persons of the divine Trinity, we now have a hope that will not put us to shame—either now or in the life to come.

If you have not come to this place, then think on these things. Neither you nor anyone else will understand all of this exhaustively. But we can have substantial knowledge. We can come to a place where we know enough to make a com-mitment. When you have enough to go on, do ask Jesus Christ to come into your life. Everything will change. You'll never regret it.

FIVE ✐

THE PREMISE
OF TRUTH

How can I know for sure? This haunting question is constantly reinforced by the surrounding culture. We saw that the assumptions of our culture need to be challenged. We saw that the center of God's revelation is the "God-man" Jesus Christ. But what if questions remain? Where can we find confirmation of this revelation? Is there a record we can consult when we need clarity?

I AM WITH YOUR MOUTH

Revelation means lifting the veil. But there is something deceptive about putting it that way. In a sense, it is not we who must cleverly lift the veil that hides the truth after a long search. Rather, the initiative must come from above. To be sure, it is we who must respond in faith. That is our part of the bargain. But faith is a response, not an initiative. We lift up empty hands to the God who is there. He is the one who gets through to us, despite the veil of our own making.

Woody Allen once said that he could believe in God if he were given a clear sign, such as a large sum of money deposited in his bank account! More seriously, the twentieth-century philosopher and skeptic Bertrand Russell was once asked what he might say to God, should he meet him after death. "Not enough evidence," Russell replied. But is that really so?

Jewish and Christian religion claims that God has been present in human affairs, engaged in the fabric of world history. The technical term for this is *theophany*—literally, the manifestation of God. Though he is transcendent, far off, totally other, he is also and at the same time close at hand, immanent, here with us. Though the original close friendship between God and humanity, reflected in the story of the Garden of Eden in Genesis, was broken, he still comes to bring reconciliation. Inasmuch as the whole purpose of creation was put at risk because of this broken relationship, God, in his love, set about to restore the bond.

This is radical and unique. Unlike the teaching found in any of the world's religions, the biblical account tells not of our reaching up, but of God's reaching down to humanity by special revelation. The great philosophies and the religions of the world have it the other way: somehow we must struggle to lift the veil and find a way to overcome our earthly limitations. While there is much wisdom in the world religions, there is this crucial place where biblical religion differs from other approaches. The Old and New Testaments relate how the Lord God made himself known by theophanies, in a progressive order of intensity, until the great, incomparable theophany of Jesus Christ.

There are a number of forms of God's intervention in human affairs. Very early, God appeared to the patriarchs as a messenger. For example, Abraham met three mysterious visitors who told him he would have a child in his old age. He called them "lord" and bowed down to them (Genesis 18:2–3). A bit later in the Old Testament we read of the powerful presence of God in the fire and cloud that accompanied Israel. The Lord showed himself specially in the worship of the Jews. This occurred first in the tabernacle, a sort of movable sanctuary, then in the temple, a glorious permanent structure. The problem of a transcendent God inhabiting a building did not elude the people of Israel. But they knew that somehow his presence was an act of mercy, one that signaled a relationship between God and his people, and so they accepted it by faith.

At the dedication of the first temple, Solomon's prayer shows this understanding:

> But will God really dwell on earth with men? The heavens, even the highest heavens, cannot contain you. How much less this temple I have built! Yet give attention to your servant's prayer and his plea for mercy, O LORD my God. Hear the cry and the prayer that your servant is praying in your presence. (2 Chronicles 6:18–19)

At the close of this prayer, the record shows that fire from heaven came down and consumed the sacrifices prepared for the ceremony. The temple was so filled with the cloud of the glory of God that the priests couldn't enter the place. But rather than terror, this theophany engendered praise and thanksgiving, for the people bowed down to worship, saying, "He is good; his love endures forever" (2 Chronicles 7:3).

There were other kinds of theophanies in the Old Testament. They are all precursors to the final theophany, the supreme one. In the first century of the common era, Jesus Christ descended to earth as a human being, as we have already seen. The gospel of John describes this amazing incarnation of the Son of God by echoing the first words of the Bible:

> In the beginning was the Word, and the Word was with God, and the word was God. . . . The Word became flesh and made his dwelling among us. (John 1:1, 14)

The word translated "made his dwelling" among us is the same word for "tabernacle." In other words, Jesus Christ, who was there in the beginning, who is in fact God, became the final version of that movable tent of worship described earlier. Jesus Christ, God's Son, was incarnate.

The incarnation is sometimes known as the "grand miracle." Jesus Christ is the ultimate exhibit of revealed religion. He is the culmination of all the prophetic utterances of old. Many of them were spoken, and some (the most significant) were written. Of course, God also made himself known in visions from time to time. Dreams were sometimes the vehicle for revelation in the Old Testament. Most often, though, God revealed himself through the speech of prophets and apostles.

The spoken form was given over a period of centuries. But how could the infinite God break into our finitude and speak clearly? What guarantee do we have that the Bible is God's revelation and not simply human speculation? How do we know it is not mere legend?

We are not told a great deal about the exact method of the revelation to the prophets. Instead, we are given a set of presuppositions by which we can fully understand how God does get through. There is a telling incident in the book of Exodus (chapters 3–4). We alluded to it briefly, but let's take a closer look.

After some very hard years of Israel's slavery in Egypt, the Lord appeared to Moses, their deliverer. We have here a dramatic theophany, for the angel of the Lord appeared in flames of fire from within a bush. It is called the burning bush, because though it was on fire, it was not consumed.

This is a pregnant symbol. The bush was a humble thornbush, not a lofty tree. It represented Israel in its humility, despised by the Egyptian slave drivers. The fire was not so much the source of light. (It was the other way around: God, the light produced the fire.) The fire represented the damaging force of burning. Indeed, Israel was being burned in the furnace of affliction. Yet the bush was not consumed. That is, since the God of mercy was the source of the fire, his people were being refined, chastened, but not destroyed. Furthermore, Israel was about to become the instrument of God's judgment against its oppressors. That fire would destroy and consume the tyrants. God was calling Moses to be the leader in this action of emancipation.

God had revealed himself to Moses as "the God of your father, the God of Abraham, the God of Isaac and the God of Jacob" (Exodus 3:6) He was to go challenge the pharaoh and bring the people out of Egypt. Somewhat understandably, after gaining his composure, Moses expressed some reservations about his abilities to be God's man. The first was that he did not have the right qualifications: "Who am I, that I should go to Pharaoh and bring the Israelites out of Egypt?" (Exodus 3:11). God answered that he would be with him, and safely bring them all back to this very place. Moses then objected that the people would need further information on God's name. The name was crucial in ancient cultures, for it signified the identity and the accomplishments of its bearer. God answered with those enigmatic words, "I AM WHO I AM," a play on the Hebrew word for being (Exodus 3:14).

This revelation was most likely not a statement about God's pure, self-defining being, although that may be true enough. The God of Aristotle had that much going for him. It was more likely a way to tell Moses that his question was off base. Defining God is not so important as knowing him. He had been faithful in the past and for that reason could be counted on for the future. His actual name was *I am*. God told Moses to say to the Israelites, "I AM has sent me to you" (Exodus 3:14).

God then promised to give Moses the power to perform certain miracles of judgment against the Egyptians, because he knew they would not believe him. Moses, still not sure, asked for proof (Exodus 4:1). The Lord gave him some examples right then and there. Finally—and this is most important—Moses objected that he was not a good speaker. In the Hebrew, his line is something like, "I am not much with words, because my mouth and my tongue are heavy" (Exodus 4:10). The exact nature of his disability is not certain. He might have had a speech impediment. He might have been out of practice with Egyptian, having spent so many years away. Or, he could simply have been making excuses. Whatever the case, God answered in an intriguing way:

> *Who gave man his mouth? Who makes him deaf or mute? Who gives him sight or makes him blind? Is it not I, the* LORD*? Now go; I will help you speak and will teach you what to say. (Exodus 4:11–12)*

The more literal translation is significant. After establishing his utter sovereignty over the human body, God added that he would help him speak. Verse 12 literally means, "I am with your mouth." Neither Moses nor we should have missed the philosophy that makes revelation possible: God made the mouth, and he can use it to speak divine words. For that matter, the name of God contains not only a philosophy, but a heart—God's heart. He would exercise all the faithfulness needed to accomplish this otherwise impossible task: I am, that is, the faithful one, would do this.

YOUR WORD IS TRUTH

We are dealing here with what makes revelation possible. I remember being witness to a discussion between a believer and an unbeliever. The skeptic had serious doubts about the virgin birth of Jesus Christ. His arguments were several, centering mostly on the fact that a virgin birth is a biological impossibility. The biblical accounts were so many myths to him, spun by credulous people.

After various retorts the believer finally took things to a more foundational level. On naturalistic presuppositions, virgin births are indeed impossible. But what if those presuppositions were wrong? What if there were a Creator God, one who had formed the entire human race and had specifically endowed human beings with their extraordinary reproductive system? How difficult would it be for this God, in this one instance, when a special birth was in view, to circumvent the role of the male, and produce a supernatural conception in the woman? The conversation then took on a decidedly different tone. The skeptic began to see that the issue was not this or that law of nature, but the existence of a powerful God.

The most complete and final form of these utterances is the Bible. The Scriptures of the Old and New Testaments are not simply a record of theophanies, though they certainly are that. Nor are they only a collection of the best or most significant utterances of the prophets and apostles. They are themselves a revelation. When God planned the redemption of humankind, he ensured that a document would be produced that contained all that was necessary for us to know him. For it to serve that purpose, it had to be a revealed text. As one passage puts it, "All Scripture is God-breathed and is useful for teaching, rebuking, correcting and training in righteousness" (2 Timothy 3:16).

The text of Scripture did not simply come down from heaven in a large volume. It was given in many ways and on many occasions. Various texts no doubt existed from very ancient times. But the first significant grouping, known as the Pentateuch (we divide it into five books), was given and then consolidated around the time of Israel's exodus from Egypt. This portion is called the Torah, meaning law or instruction, because it carries the fundamental ordinances of God to Israel at the time in its history when it was constituted a people. Subsequent portions were produced during the significant events of the life of that people. Then, the final deposit came surrounding the coming of Jesus Christ and the foundation of the new Israel, the church.

All these different portions of Scripture belong together. They were never meant to be considered alone or isolated from one another. Thus, over time, the various books were combined. Though diverse and varied, each portion is part of a whole, so that we legitimately have one word for the group: the Bible (the "book"). This unity is ensured because of the unique source. God is the primary author of the Bible, even though he used human beings as its vehicles. As someone has put it, it is the Word of the Lord, because he is the Lord of the Word.

The Bible is not simply a history book recording events in narratives. Nor is it only a collection of commandments and wise sayings. It is a covenant book. That is, the Bible is a constitution. It establishes who God is and how he has acted redemptively in history, supremely in Jesus Christ, and then it enjoins us to faith and allegiance. As one theologian has explained, the Scripture is

> not merely a narrative of what happened years ago, but the perennial speech of God to man. . . . It forms a lasting bond of union between heaven and earth, between Christ and His Church, and between God and His people. In it we hear ever anew the voice of God, for it remains the inspired Word of God.[1]

Special revelation through Christ is thus confirmed and established by the Bible.

It works the other way around. Jesus Christ is the clear confirmation of the Bible. The Lord of the Word gives the biblical message its great clarity and beauty. The Lord who first appeared to the apostles, confirming his Word to them, will finally appear to the whole world, openly, in great splendor. That will be the final proof of what we now see only "through a glass darkly" (1 Corinthians 13:12 KJV). But today we have enough, more than enough, to believe and to conform our lives to God's special revelation.

> And we have the word of the prophets made more certain, and you will do well to pay attention to it, as to a light

shining in a dark place, until the day dawns and the morning star rises in your hearts. (2 Peter 1:19)

To be sure, this does not settle all the questions. The Bible is not only God's Word, but a human document, as we have noted. It was not given by dictation, like the Qu'ran, but composed through the instrumentality of men and women over a long period of time. Furthermore, it has not come to us in the form of the original autographs, presuming they even existed. Instead, we have manuscripts—copies based on the originals—with certain variants. And, of course, most of us read the Bible not in the original languages—Hebrew, Aramaic, and Greek—but in translation. Even the New Testament authors used a translation of the Old Testament for their quotes. And there appear to be contradictions within the different accounts.

This is not the place to explore the many questions raised by the humanity of Scripture. Suffice it to say, there are good and sufficient answers for many of these problems. More importantly, there are deeper reasons why we need not answer all of the questions in order to arrive at the certainty of biblical inspiration.

According to its own wisdom, the Bible is not always easy to understand. Consider the apostle Peter's statement about the letters of his colleague, the apostle Paul:

Paul also wrote you with the wisdom that God gave him. He writes the same way in all his letters, speaking in them of these matters [about God's patience leading to peace with him]. His letters contain some things that are hard to understand, which ignorant and unstable people distort, as they do the other Scriptures, to their own destruction. (2 Peter 3:15–16)

Harsh words, yet to the point. Not everything is clear or easy to understand. That makes some things open to distortion. Yet the wisdom of God does get through. The Bible is clear enough to serve God's purposes. If this were not the case, then God would have failed to provide all we need for the purposes of his mercy toward us. We could not respond in faith, because we would not know what we needed to know (see Romans 10:8, paraphrasing Deuteronomy 30:12).

Why would God give us a Bible that is not altogether clear? One reason Scripture "has its own secrets," as Francis Turretin reminds us, is "to control human pride, and to purge the contempt that easily could have arisen from too much ease of understanding."[2] But the fundamental reason is this. If everything were quite clear to us, then how could the Bible be the Word of a transcendent God? "Now we see but a poor reflection as in a mirror; then we shall see face to face" (1 Corinthians 13:12). Still, because God is the Father of lights, he gets through the darkness. "In your light we see light," says Psalm 36:9.

This balance, knowing what we need to know, but not having exhaustive clarity, has never been better expressed than in the seventeenth-century church document, the Westminster Confession of Faith:

> All things in scripture are not alike plain in themselves, nor alike clear unto all; yet those things which are necessary to be known, believed, and observed, for salvation, are so clearly propounded and opened in some place of scripture or other, that not only the learned, but the unlearned, in a due sense of the ordinary means, may attain unto a sufficient understanding of them. (1.7)

Not only that, but it is actually better to have the written, prophetic word, than a lot of dramatic signs. Contrary to what Woody Allen professed, there are certain dangers in receiving special signs. John Calvin explained:

> Now daily oracles are not sent from heaven, for it pleased the Lord to hallow his truth to everlasting remembrance in the Scriptures alone [cf. John 5:39]. Hence the Scriptures obtain full authority among believers only when men regard them as having sprung from heaven, as if there the living words of God were heard. (Institutes 1.7.1)

Ironically, of course, Woody Allen has had numerous large amounts of money deposited in his bank account. As far as we can tell, it hasn't convinced him of God's truth. Ironically too, Bertrand Russell would have a hard time claiming the lack of evidence before God. He just didn't want to see it. He did not care to read the pages and regard them as having sprung from heaven.

The record is there for anyone to consult. If the external world is not enough for you, then look at Jesus Christ. If that is not enough, then search the Scriptures. If that is not enough, your problem is not evidence. It is attitude.

SIX 🖋

COLLISION COURSE

I s this Bible a verifiable document? How can we trust a book so ancient? Doesn't it contain numerous contradictions? Is it not culture-bound? Has science not refuted the accuracy of the Scriptures?

THE BIBLE VERSUS ARISTOTLE

There has been a long history of quarrels between science and religion. A careful look at the issues reveals far fewer real conflicts than is sometimes imagined. Conflicts did occur and still do, of course, but it is urgent that we sort out the facts from some of the myths generated in popular sources.

For example, many of us have a vivid image of the Roman Catholic Church in the seventeenth century standing in opposition to Galileo's defense of a sun-centered system. Through popular literature, we recall a famous trial where Galileo's book the *Dialogue*, with its pro-Copernican position, was banned, and the elderly scientist was put under house arrest. Unfortunately, because of the volatile atmosphere surrounding that debate (and others since), as well as the political implications, it is not always easy to sort out the legitimate questions from the emotional ones. Nor do some of the serious attempts at working out the problems get the attention they deserve. The widely held impression of a conflict between religion and science is a mixture of truth and error.

Consider the actual events and points of view in the Galileo affair. In hindsight, June 21, 1633, was not a good day for the church. On that date, the last action was taken in a trial sponsored by the Holy Office in Rome, one in which Galileo was summoned for his final interrogation. The Jesuit priests had been quite active in bringing this matter to a head. After considerable debate and controversy, Galileo was officially accused of promulgating the Copernican view, which put the sun at the center and suggested that the earth orbited around it.

This view had two flaws, the Holy Office maintained. The first was that it had not been supported by sufficient evidence. The second was that it was incompatible with the Bible. Much of the substance for this accusation was drawn from the *Dialogue,* a major book in which Galileo had tried to present both sides—the older Aristotelian model and the newer astronomy. Despite his attempts to show the strengths and weaknesses of both cosmologies, he had clearly sympathized with the newer approach. He offered as one major argument the pattern of the ocean tides, which could only be explained by the moon orbiting the earth. But this was not convincing to the Holy Office.

This condemnation would have tremendous consequences for the future of relations between the church and the scientific community. Galileo received a harsh punishment despite what he thought would be an out of court settlement. He had agreed to recant the "errors and heresies" of a sun-centered system. This was all the more tragic in that he had put forth the theory in good faith, believing it to be compatible with a true reading of Scripture. Many people regard the church's denunciation as paradigmatic of a repressive bigotry that would continue to resist free inquiry over the generations.

The real story is more complex. Galileo had invested much of his professional career crusading for the right of the natural sciences to explore theories that might not always please the reigning philosophies, whether in the academy or in the church. He was himself a committed churchman, however, and looked for ways to build bridges between science and theology. Though clearly a controversialist and somewhat prone to aggravate his enemies, his basic battle was against neither Rome nor the Jesuit priests who had evidently stalked him until he could be brought to trial. Nor was his battle against the Bible, which he believed was quite compatible with the newer cosmology. His battle was against the prevailing Aristotelian worldview, one which required the earth to be at the center of the physical universe, surrounded by a number of revolving spheres, which explained the movement of the planets. The stars were moved by an aspiration of the first cause, the "unmoved mover."

The greatest medieval theologian was the Dominican Thomas Aquinas (1225–74). His theology was strongly influenced by Aristotle, who was being rediscovered at that time through certain Arabic philosophers. In the thirteenth century, the Roman Church did not on the whole look favorably at Aristotle's philosophy. Indeed, in 1277 several of

Thomas Aquinas's teachings were condemned by the universities of Paris and Oxford, which held considerable sway, because of their dependence upon Aristotle. Things would change in the fourteenth century, partly because of the efforts of the Dominicans. Thomas was canonized in 1323, and from then on Aristotelianism regained favor. By the time of Galileo, though it was being challenged here and there, the Aristotelian approach was still regnant.

Aristotle's philosophy was nothing less than a monumental achievement. Not only was it comprehensive, covering almost every aspect of inquiry from ethics to logic to metaphysics, but it was coherent, presenting a well-ordered system of thought wherein all the pieces held together. One can readily understand the attraction of this system for theologians in the Middle Ages, who were drawn for many reasons to order and balance.

Think of the great churches, especially the Gothic cathedrals, with their scrupulously proportioned floors and their high walls and steeples reaching to heaven. Though a pre-Christian Greek thinker, Aristotle had so many elements that appeared compatible with the requirements of symmetry and categorization in theology that a sort of marriage between the two had been effected. He wrote about laws of logic, such as noncontradiction, going from known truths to unknown, and making definitions. He listed different kinds of beings, using distinctions such as substance, quality, quantity, position, and passion. Science, he held, is universal. We can discover things by induction, using the senses. In his system, the earth was at the center of the universe. It was surrounded by different spheres. The outermost spheres were the stars, moved by the breath of God.

Aristotle's philosophy can be compared and contrasted

with that of the other great thinker from ancient Greece, Plato. Recall the extraordinary painting by Raphael, *The School of Athens*. In it, Plato lifts his finger toward the skies, but Aristotle points downward, toward the earth. Plato spoke of the *idea*, but Aristotle spoke of the *form*. Whereas Plato thought of the universe as *history*, Aristotle thought of it as *system*. Plato wanted to know where things came from and where they were going. Aristotle was more interested in whether things exist and what their composition is.

This was a powerful model, one the church was drawn to, one that a genius like Thomas Aquinas would attempt to combine with a theological system. Aristotle gave the medieval church logical arts to use in its arguments for the faith. He gave it a beautiful cosmology to describe as God's speech to the human race. He gave the church an anthropology to use in explaining the image of God. He gave the church an argument for the existence of an unmoved mover to use as proof of the Creator God. No wonder his system was attractive.

In its battles with Galileo, then, the early modern Roman Catholic Church understood that a new astronomy would be a serious blow dealt against this entire worldview. To threaten this one piece, the planetary system, was to threaten the whole. A lot was at stake.

Political and personal questions were involved as well. In this case, Pope Urban VIII, who would eventually become a key player in the condemnation of Galileo, was embroiled in various controversies that, despite having nothing to do with science, helped sway him against Galileo. He had been secretly allied to the Protestant king of Sweden, which, when discovered, brought resentment against the pope. He also had become manipulated by Richelieu, the powerful French cardinal who succeeded in protecting French sovereignty from

Rome. Things were not going well at home, either. The pope's enemies accused him of using his office to promote his family. He became somewhat paranoid.

So here was a chance to vindicate the church, and to show strength against the threat of heresy—a good reason to condemn Galileo, whatever the merits or demerits of his case.

It is true that Galileo was dealt with rather harshly. But it is not true that his views were completely silenced and that he had to live as a prisoner. Even after his condemnation, he was given considerable freedom to continue to work against the Aristotelian paradigm. He would write a set of *Discourses*, which would pave the way toward some of Newton's views.

SCRIPTURE LIBERATES THE CREATION

It should be noted that the church at this time did not have a united voice. The body that condemned Galileo was the Roman Catholic Church. There was a growing *Protestant* church that had been forced to break away from the main Western branch of Catholicism over issues such as papal corruption, justification by faith, and scriptural authority. Protestantism was more open to the kinds of views held by Galileo. It moved faster toward the divorce with Aristotle than did the Roman Church.

There is good reason to believe that John Calvin, the great Genevan Reformer from the previous generation, was familiar with some of Copernicus's work and was open to accepting its principles of planetary motion. Calvin's approach to the book of Genesis can be described as accommodationist. That is, he believed that though the text was absolutely authoritative, its descriptions of the world were not always couched in the technical language of science, but often in the more phenomenological language of the simple believer. Genesis is, as he called it, "a book for laymen," and should not be used to test particular schools of contemporary astronomy.

Living in the same era as Galileo, the Dutch Protestant minister and first-rate astronomer, Philips van Lansbergen (1561–1632), staunchly defended the Copernican view. His belief was that "Scripture is given by inspiration of God, and is profitable for doctrine, for reproof, for correction, for instruction in righteousness, but it is not meet for instruction in geometry and astronomy."[1]

Protestants were not all free from Aristotle, to be sure. But their general approach to testing all things from Scripture had the effect of liberating them from the monumental Thomistic synthesis.

In sum, the Galileo affair happened because of a combination of circumstances. Future skeptics would point to the incident as proof of the church's authoritarian wariness against progress, scientific or otherwise. This is simply not the case.

First of all, the whole notion of progress is itself a loaded concept. It comes from an Enlightenment ideal about human reason being the key to the future. It is true that the church was not anxious to give everything up in favor of unaided reason. But there was plenty of room for the exercise of reason. Second, the whole complex system of baptized Aristotelianism we've just described was far more the product of human reason than of careful study of Scripture. Thus, the church was not so much afraid of "progress" as it was concerned to safeguard the assumed convergence between Aristotle and theology and not give in to unbridled reason.

This would of course prove misguided. Thomas Aquinas

had not put Aristotle carefully to the test—the test of Scripture. The marriage of Aristotle and theology was in that sense unfortunate. There would have to be a divorce. Galileo was one of the voices in favor of that eventual divorce.

It is too bad history tends to remember such admittedly regrettable examples as Galileo's conflict with the church when in fact Christian faith had a great deal to do with the *rise* of modern science. The story of the role of biblically informed believers and the growth of Western science has been told many times. Certainly no simple relation of cause and effect could do justice to that story. It would be gross simplification to imagine scientists with their Bibles in hand, observing the natural world to find its God-given patterns and laws. Yet it is true that the mentality gained in the sixteenth and seventeenth centuries from a new respect for the text of the Scripture lent itself to more unbiased observation.

A case in point is the "secularization" of the creation. The medieval and early Renaissance worldviews tended to endow physical objects with a soul, and miracles were expected constantly in the natural realm. This began to change when the biblical doctrine of the world as God's creation was taken to mean something less mechanical than Aristotle's system. Genesis describes a process whereby the world was made in six days, each day contributing to a more habitable place. Earlier, Augustine had believed that the universe came into being instantaneously. But now, as Christians began to take Genesis chapter 1 more seriously as a text, they saw the possibility of at least a limited progression over time. The idea of progression within the creation week may seem a small step to take, but it was a critical step, because it dared to question Augustine, the most revered church father.

The process set in motion would soon lead considerably

beyond what the text of Genesis might warrant. How expositors eventually allowed for a concordance between Genesis 1 and large-scale evolutionary schemes is another story, a complex one at that. But in Galileo's day the battle was over whether the world was an Aristotelian machine with a sacred hue or a created order, the *earth* whose inhabitants both dwell there and freely explore its riches. In a certain sense, then, a sun-centered system meant a sort of demythologizing. Thus exorcised, the natural realm became a safe place to explore. Miracles were still believed, but they were not thought to occur every day.

The great poet Petrarch was said to be the first person to climb a mountain for the simple pleasure of arriving at the top! More profoundly, many of the great revolutionary scientists were motivated by Christian principles. William Turner, Gabriel Harvey, Francis Bacon, Johannes Kepler, and, of course, Isaac Newton himself were all deeply committed to the idea that the glory of God could be discovered in the patterns of the surrounding world.

If the Galileo affair centered on the larger struggle to move from an Aristotelian to a post-Aristotelian worldview, that does not by any means signify that the succeeding paradigm was either final and objective or biblically warranted. With the rise of Newton's approach, a clearly mathematical, somewhat mechanistic view of the universe would emerge. Though on the surface it was more compatible with the Bible, it had its own problems. Much later, the general theory of relativity would displace the Newtonian model.

So, then, it is quite true that conflicts have occurred between science and religion. They still do. But in every case there is far more to the story than meets the eye. When it ignites, the conflict is rarely between something so monolithic as "science" and something so uniform as "the church." There are almost always political, academic, and philosophical aspects that entered the picture and lend their influence.

Honesty requires us to say two things. First, serious mistakes are made at times. Christians have jumped to conclusions, defended the wrong things, or misunderstood the Bible. But second, there has been far more positive interaction between the realms of faith and science than we tend to acknowledge. To speak historically, so fruitful was the cross-pollination at the dawn of the modern era, it can truly be said that without Christian beliefs we simply would not have modern science as we know it.

SCRIPTURE LIBERATES THE SCRIPTURE

The relationship between science and faith is like the relationship between two neighboring countries. At times they are allies. That is the scenario they both hope for. It is the way things should be. Science, which looks at God's world, should not be in conflict with theology, which looks at the Bible. But at times conflict sets in. The countries find reasons to quarrel. Some disputes can be settled by arbitration. Occasionally, though, they go to war.

When that happens, not every citizen necessarily agrees with his mother country. One side may be mostly in the right, or both sides may be quite wrong. Thomas Aquinas's synthesis of faith with Aristotle had certain strengths and produced many good things. But in fundamental ways it was seriously flawed. The theologians of the church were thus locked in, preventing science from moving beyond Aristotle to a more reasonable view.

The collision could have been avoided had both sides been more willing to look for common ground. That could only have happened if there were more humility and more tentativeness about cosmologies. The Bible is God's Word, but it does not present an iron-clad, timeless cosmology, one that fits in with a particular philosophy. It is not that kind of book. It's a covenant book. Certainly it speaks truly even when it touches on areas that are considered the domain of science. But it is not a science textbook and must not be read as though it were. And it must be honored for the text that it is.

When I was a high school student, we had a religion course in which the instructor assured us that we could no longer believe the biblical account of the world. The reason is that the biblical account has the earth as the foundation. Ancient peoples believed that human beings were the center of everything. Further, the biblical account speaks of a three-decker universe, with the heavens above, the earth at our level, and the ocean below. Clearly, he taught us, this ancient view has been dispelled by "science."

It was only years later, when I decided to read the Bible for myself, that I realized things were not as my teacher had said. According to the Bible, the earth is not a foundation, though it is created, like everything else in the universe. Nor does Scripture put humankind at the center. God is at the center. Certainly the main activity described by the Bible is on earth. The whole story of redemption is about human beings, not other beings, not even angels. So of course the earth is at the "center" in this sense.

But there is no biblical idea whatsoever of a three-decker universe. When occasionally three-decker language is used, it is simply to describe the big picture, not to establish a contrived earth-centered cosmology. It's an obvious anthropomorphic perspective from which most of us operate on a daily basis. The Bible is no more a commitment to a particular cosmology than a navigator who charts a ship's location based on the sun and the stars "out there."

When the biblical writers meditate on the creation, they are not speculating on the laws of physics. They are not attempting a unified field theory. With respect to the cosmos, as Calvin noted, there is undoubtedly accommodation going on. No, the biblical authors, rather, are in awe of the wonder, the vastness of it all. They are struck by the insignificance of the human creature:

> When I consider your heavens,
>   the work of your fingers,
> the moon and the stars,
>   which you have set in place,
> what is man that you are mindful of him,
>   the son of man that you care for him? (Psalm 8:3–4)

This is the furthest thing from a man-centered world. It does answer the question, though:

> You have made him a little lower than the heavenly beings
>   and crowned him with glory and honor. (verse 5)

But the writer is rather astonished at this, not complacent. Whatever cosmology the Bible may contain, it is nothing that "science" has to reject, or replace with something more enlightened. Observations of the natural world are meant to drive us to worship the Creator.

Perhaps the heart of the message in these considerations is this: Humility, gratitude, worship, will do more to bring reconciliation where it is needed between the Bible and scientific work than any other practice. Test yourself to see if these are your heart commitments. Some issues are hard, and much work needs to be done. But faith and science are ultimately friends, if we'll only go about them honestly.

SEVEN ☞

SCIENCE ON TRIAL

Of all the stumbling blocks to believing the Bible, few have had more impact than evolutionary theory. Recall the gravitational pull to the question of origins at the young student's thesis defense. Does it matter how we got here? Why should anyone care how things began? Could God not have used evolution to create? Should we not simply and humbly remain agnostic about theories of origins?

WHO IS A FUNDAMENTALIST?

Appeals to humility and tentativeness should never mean avoiding issues. Whereas the Galileo affair raised the question of the compatibility of the Bible with Aristotle, neither side in the debate questioned the role of the Creator. Evolutionary theory does. In the seventeenth-century trial no one questioned the Bible, let alone God's creative activity. In a famous twentieth-century trial both were at issue.

It occurred in the summer of 1925 in Dayton, Tennessee, and centered on the prosecution of a young science teacher. John T. Scopes had taught a class on human evolution despite a state law against it. Though such laws were rarely enforced, circumstances converged to turn this into a test case for the much larger issue of "science" and "religion." Was Darwinism fact? Was it theory? Was it anti-Christian? Could it be reconciled with the Bible?

Two of the best legal minds in the country were brought in to debate these questions: Clarence Darrow, perhaps the greatest living criminal lawyer in America and staunch atheist, and William Jennings Bryan, the fiery evangelical politician and orator. Thus the relatively insignificant infraction of a state law on curriculum became a pretext for much bigger questions troubling America at the time. The whole thing took on mythic proportions. Every paper reported on it, and it was known as "the trial of the century."

If one were to believe only the account given by the play, made into a film, *Inherit the Wind*, or the more academic report by Ray Ginger, *Six Days of Forever?*, the tacit conclusion would be that this "summer for the gods" spelled the end of fundamentalist credibility. A discouraged and embarrassed dragon, William Jennings Bryan, had been slain by the ruthless debating Saint George, Clarence Darrow. Literalistic fundamentalism lost; scientific honesty won. Freedom of speech gained victory over obscurantist repression.

But, once again, the facts are nothing quite so one-sided. Bryan was certainly a "fundamentalist." This loaded word has a rather fascinating history. The term was coined in 1920 by a conservative Baptist in America who wanted to fight for the fundamentals of the faith, over against "modernism," a more flexible version. "Fundamentalism" soon came to refer to many groups within the more militant branch of the evangelical Protestant church. There was considerable diversity among fundamentalists, but there was essential agreement on such doctrines as the inerrancy of Scripture, the virgin birth of Christ, his death and physical resurrection, and his personal and visible return at the end of history.

Fundamentalism was the heir to the grand tradition of American evangelicalism from the previous century. That tradition included gospel-preaching fervor, social reform, activist women's movements, mass evangelism, and a strong emphasis on education. By the 1930s, and from then on, fundamentalists were separatists. They tended to reject ecumenism and in general to fear all that might resemble world federation.

"Modernism" was an imprecise term that generally meant liberal Christianity, including a critical view of the Bible, and willingness to question the fundamental doctrines, including the physical resurrection. Modernism should not be confused with modernity. Though by the 1920s the fundamentalists had a decided antimodernist outlook, that in no way meant they opposed all that was carried on the wave of modernity, especially in such areas as science and politics. Many fundamentalists in fact were fervent about science and anxious to prove the historicity of the Bible with the help of scientific research.

One of the problems here, ironically, was that they often accepted certain premises about science that stemmed from the Enlightenment, premises that science itself would eventually call into serious question. So, for example, there were all kinds of books that tried to show how factual the gospel was, how scientifically valid was the resurrection, naïvely resting their case on autonomous reason and evidence in the form of supposedly neutral brute facts.

William Jennings Bryan was indeed a fundamentalist. But his opposition to Darwinism was not simply because it seemed incompatible with the Genesis account of Creation. Nor only because it was often held by atheists. His basic disagreement was because he feared it could lead to social Darwinism. Bryan was a populist. He was on a constant crusade for the rights of people from the grassroots. He especially wanted them to be free from the tyranny of the expert. He saw Darwinism as a "menace" out to destroy Christian faith. It was both unscientific and unpersuasive. Most of all, it violates the rights of parents to have their children taught the truth of Creation. He supported state laws against the teaching of evolution because he believed evolution was a theory—and a false one—being presented as fact.

Contrary to the impression he has given to posterity, Bryan did not want public schools to inculcate Christian faith to students. He believed in a separation of church and state that would also preclude the book of Genesis being taught. His worry was that an elite minority would begin to control the general population.

In point of fact, Bryan's own views were surprisingly congruent with certain aspects of Darwinism. For example, he accepted the longer geological timetable required by evolution. Like many other Christians—fundamentalist or not—he believed that the "days" of Genesis chapter 1 were in fact "eons," or ages. He allowed that there could have been evolution before the creation of human beings. It was not so much the particulars of evolutionary theory that he distrusted. Rather, it was the larger question of the nefarious attack of evolutionary philosophy against civilization.

For proof, he looked at a famous survey of college students conducted by Bryn Mawr professor James Leuba, which showed a decline in their faith over the four years of their college experience. That decline was, according to the study, directly correlated to the courses they took in natural science. Indeed, it was further revealed that some two-thirds of American biologists believed in neither a personal God nor the immortality of the soul.

Clarence Darrow himself had come from an intellectual heritage of enmity against biblical religion. From the first time Darwin's *Origin of Species* was published in Great Britain (1859), there had been philosophers and scientists willing to use it as the ultimate weapon against traditional Christianity. T. H. Huxley was perhaps the most famous of the Victorian polemicists against Christian faith. He took on bishop Wilberforce in 1860, in a debate that had little to do with real science and everything to do with a clash of worldviews. Huxley believed Christianity was built on a clerical elite and held thinking people back from the freedom of inquiry. Wilberforce believed Darwin's views would lead to an intolerable battleground of raw, godless power.

In the Scopes trial, Darrow focused on the most difficult aspects of biblical literalism, such as the size of the fish that swallowed Jonah, the creation of Eve out of Adam's rib, and the sun standing still for Joshua. He did not, of course, allow Bryan to play his strengths: his biblical theology as a foundation for the dignity of humans as God's image-bearers, the high calling of each individual under God's providence, and the great hope furnished by the resurrection of Christ. Darrow's only purpose, as he would himself put it, was to "show the country what an ignoramus [Bryan] was *and I succeeded.*"[1]

In the end, the state law was upheld. Scopes was fined. But a sea change had occurred. Bryan died five days later, whether from exhaustion or discouragement, we don't know. A brief was soon filed against the anti-evolution law, and the state supreme court rendered a complex decision basically preventing the legality of the law ever really being tested, and having the effect of overturning Scopes's conviction. The fundamentalists had won the battle but lost the war.

NATURAL LAW TO THE RESCUE?

What about the issue itself? What about Genesis and evolution? The issue is loaded with land mines. Both sides— the humanist and the Christian—tend to confuse the real issues. Carl Sagan's television series *Cosmos*, aired a number of years ago, was the quintessence of militant humanism. At the center was his provocative statement, "The cosmos is all there is, there was, or ever will be." Some fundamentalists are no better, with no interest in exploring what the text of Genesis could mean other than as a bastion against evolutionary theory. There are churches that make holding to a 144-hour creation week (six twenty-four–hour days) a test of genuine faith. Do we have to choose between 15 billion years and 144 hours? Is our only option Darrow or Bryan?

Let's consider both sides of the discussion. First, the scientific side: Are not parts of evolutionary theory seriously flawed? Clarence Darrow was confident it all held together. Today, very few of the actual dynamics put forth by Charles Darwin have remained believable. A centerpiece of his view is the survival of the fittest. This has a surface plausibility. When you look at certain birds with long beaks digging for food, you can easily imagine a process whereby the bird best able to get food in hard places would outlive the ones that couldn't. Yet the survival of the fittest (by differential birth, or death) has been contested not only by theists but also by naturalists.

One of the most serious obstacles to accepting a simple, linear progression of species is what is called irreducible complexity. To get to the final product, each step along the way has to have its own *raison d'être*, yet be less adequate than the final product. For example, to arrive at the eye, there must be separate reasons for the different parts of the eye to be selected, then surpassed, on the way to the eye as we know it. But that is not the case. Why would a retina exist without a lens, an optic nerve, and so on. And what sorts of precursors to the eye might exist for a while and then not survive?

Darwin himself admitted this was a problem:

> To suppose that the eye, with all of its inimitable contrivances for adjusting the focus to different distances, for admitting different amounts of light, and for the correction of spherical and chromatic aberration, could have been formed by natural selection, seems, I freely confess, absurd in the highest possible degree.[2]

He would go on to say that nevertheless reason requires we believe some sort of evolutionary process did lead to the eye. Later theorists would try to alter the gradualism of the theory and argue for abrupt appearances of things like eyes. But all such explanations stumble over the same obstacle. How can the parts make sense without the whole?

It is something like the existence of an automobile engine. How could one explain the isolated development of a piston, or a spark plug, or a fuel line, or a crank shaft, etc., without having some notion of the whole? In other words, why would a four-wheel carriage have miscellaneous engine parts short of a whole working engine?

As soon as one admits that there is a whole in view, then design raises its head. The parts of the world are irreducibly complex. Their existence cannot be justified without a view toward the larger whole into which they purposefully fit. To change the metaphor, the parts of a watch are designed and assembled according to the whole end-product envisioned by its creator, or not at all. The watch needs a watchmaker.

Many other aspects of Darwin's theory have been questioned. But one should scarcely imagine that this means the entire theory of evolution has been abandoned. Alternate theories, which try to answer some of the problems, have been set forth. The neo-Darwinists have proposed complex genetic theories that load the chromosomes with enough potential information to explain the great diversity of species over the millennia. Stephen Jay Gould has become known for his view that things evolved by sudden jumps ("punctuated equilibrium"). But until scientists are willing to question the fundamental presupposition underlying evolutionary theory, no paradigm shift will occur.

It should therefore not be assumed that somehow by "careful scientific work," views such as autonomous evolution will crumble and creationism will emerge triumphant. This is the danger in some of the recent discussions of natural law by Christians. They are hoping that the evidence from the observed world will compellingly point to a design—so compellingly that unbelievers will be driven to conclude there is a God.

But natural law is a double-edged sword. On the one hand, it corroborates what the Bible says in many places, that the world reveals God so clearly no one can miss it (Acts

14:17; Romans 1:19–20, etc.). On the other hand, it seems to claim that we can receive that revelation and interpret it correctly without a changed heart. That is because adherents to natural law tend to think there is something ingrained in the actual substance of the world—in its laws—that could speak of the Creator even if he were not there. Though they would not all put it this way, the idea is that you can prove God from the laws of nature.

That is why so many are excited about major chinks in the armor of evolution. There is quite a network of speakers and writers going around dismantling Darwinism and then leaving it to intelligent audiences to draw their own conclusions about a Creator. A competent critique of macro-evolution and its assumptions is of some value in order to clear the ground for an acceptance of the biblical account of creation. Arriving at the conclusion that there is irreducible complexity has considerable value, no doubt. But it falls far short of proving a designer, let alone the Creator God. That is why we should hesitate to embrace full-fledged natural law arguments. Complexity does not of itself prove anything, or at least it does not prove the God of biblical revelation. He is the Creator, not merely a designer of complex patterns.

The two notions are not entirely exclusive, of course. But they differ in significant ways. The Creator speaks, and things come into being. The designer molds and shapes and helps a process along. The Creator makes the environment into a fit place for his covenant relations to his creatures. The designer sets into motion a complex of laws and structures that do not necessarily relate to human affairs. So while closed-system scientific theories such as Darwinism are full of fatal flaws, rival theories that seem to prove the Bible present their own dangers.

A similar problem emerges with other theories courted

by believers. For example, when a new consensus came along and began to replace the older "Steady State" view of the universe with the "Big Bang," many were enthusiastic because it jibed with the idea of creation. Indeed the Big Bang seemed to "prove" a beginning, which is virtually the same as proving a Creator.

But things are not so simple. Though the Big Bang sounds compatible with the idea of a Creator, does it describe the right kind of beginning? Does it prove that there was something or someone there before the beginning? Not really. How did the original, concentrated mass get there in the first place? Did it have to be God? Besides, how much overlap is there between this macro theory and the biblical account of God's making the world?

Genesis does affirm that God made the heavens and the earth, meaning that he made everything that exists. But the perspective is clearly earthly. He first called into being the *tohu wabohu*, the waste and void, which he would then gradually, day after day, mold into an earthly environment fit for human habitation. Are we really looking at comparable pictures in the Genesis account and the Big Bang? Is it apples and apples, or apples and oranges? The span of billions of years required to endorse the Big Bang theory seems so far from the biblical picture of the six days. Attempts to stretch the "days" (*yom*) of Genesis into longer periods are plausible up to a certain point but then they become awkward, to say the least.

A BETTER WAY

It would seem far wiser not to work quite so hard at harmonizing Genesis with a particular astrophysical theory of the universe. Finding flaws in reductionist theories is an important step. It can, among other things, spare the Genesis text of clashes with theories that are not so much objective paradigms but secular philosophies under scientific veneer. However, it is quite another step to harmonize a particular scientific theory with the data of Genesis.

Not that there is any ultimate contradiction between the observed world and the biblical text. The same God who reveals himself in the world also reveals himself in Scripture. The two kinds of revelation are complimentary, meant to function together. The problem is whether we try to transform a particular model, useful for certain research needs, into an all-encompassing, self-governing cosmology. Both Aristotle's and Darwin's systems were attempts to build such cosmologies. Many of the difficulties and so-called conflicts diminish when we understand this basic distinction between a useful model for a limited purpose and a totalitarian stratagem.

For example, sometimes the purpose of scientific research is best accomplished when imagining a reference point outside the earth. Thus astronomers might need to stand way outside, as it were, and look at large systems in which the earth becomes only one rotating sphere within a planetary order that itself belongs to a galaxy, which galaxy belongs to an even larger set of star systems. To do this kind of research and to propose models that best fit the data is not a *correct* understanding of the universe as opposed to the *incorrect* biblical view. It is what you have to do in order to work out certain research problems. The text of Genesis is given for a somewhat different purpose, one that in a way is no less scientific. It explains the purpose of creation, and how things went wrong.

How does it do that? Take for example the pattern in the sequence of the days in Genesis chapter 1. In the first three days of the creation God shapes the environment, and in the second three days he fashions the creatures that will live and rule in that environment. There is a lord-and-servant structure here. Much like the covenant idea, the creation is an order that allows for things to function properly in their setting.

The sun and moon (fourth day) rule over the earth where the very meaning of light is daytime (first day). The birds and the fish (fifth day) rule in the now separated skies and the water (second day). Living creatures (sixth day) rule over the freshly dried earth (third day). Human beings are made on the sixth day, but with a difference. They are God's image. They rule over the earth as a whole. And, most important, on the seventh day they rest, just as God rests. But rest does not mean inactivity. It means enjoying the finished creation. The human ruler enjoys the world and its Creator in a sabbath rest of satisfaction.

In summary, if we go to Genesis looking for data such as the distance between the earth and the sun, how photosynthesis occurred before the fourth day, and so forth, we miss the point. This first book of the Bible tells us to look at the world with a view to discovering its true purpose. It is the place God made for people—a place that has sadly gone wrong because human beings revolted against their Creator. The tragedy of this is brought home powerfully by the description of the world as a place God made in order to *benefit* human beings and to give them a supreme purpose—ruling over the earth. But they wanted it otherwise and are paying the price for their Promethean ambitions. If it were not for God's grace in Jesus Christ, who was willing to become a weakened man for our sakes, the price would be unbearable.

There is something compelling about the way the Bible can both give a satisfying picture of the world and draw us to

God's grace. There is something tragic about the way debates about Genesis, yesterday and today, have often missed that appeal altogether. In your search for God, then, be sure not to become sidetracked by the politics of these debates. The issues matter. But what matters more is whether we see the world as our place, a place that God has once again made habitable and enjoyable. The earth will one day be remade. Will you be there? Will you be in that number, when the saints go marching in?

EIGHT ❯

A CLOAK OF
DECENCY

We have managed to come a long way before introducing the problem of problems. By far the most common objection to Christian faith is the problem of evil. How can God be both good and all-powerful if evil exists? How could he let it happen?

WHY, O LORD?

The railroad train has always been a favorite image in popular music. The train moving along, down the tracks, means many things. Especially, it is a metaphor about history. It speaks of purpose; it has a teleology. The train represents hope.

Many spirituals are songs of victory, songs of salvation. Consider the old spiritual *Same Train*. It's a call to faith. This train is "blowin' at the station," the loud horn calling everyone to get aboard and to head toward heaven. It already has family members aboard. "Carry my mother, carry my sister," it says, and the implication is clear. Your family, literally or not, has already made the right decision. What about you? There is still a chance. The train will "be back tomorrow."

Back tomorrow? What about the next day? And the next? As long as we live in the present mode of history there is opportunity to get aboard the train to heaven. Someday, though, it will be the last train, and we will be forced aboard. This one will be the train of judgment. The train won't be back anymore. History will be over. The reckoning comes, and then, eternity.

Slow Train Coming is the title song from Bob Dylan's first sacred album. When he began to experiment with Christian faith, he wrote and performed this *cri de cœur* about hypocrisy in America. It was a call-and-response gospel number. The bard sang of "big time negotiators, false healers and woman haters, masters of the bluff and masters of the proposition." The refrain comes around seven times, "There's a slow, slow train coming up around the bend."

The song is hard-hitting, no doubt lacking in the subtlety of his older poetry. But it was meant to be prophetic and thus had to be clear. The song is steeped in black tradition, right down to the musical style. That day is coming, the day of reckoning that every person will have to face.

In one sense, because our time here on earth is short, this life is not significant. "Time, like an ever rolling stream, bears all our years away," says the great hymn, a paraphrase by Isaac Watts of Psalm 90. The original is mordant: "You sweep men away in the sleep of death" (verse 5).

In another sense, though, it is precisely because of the present march of history that our lives have extraordinary meaning. Though our time may be short, it is supremely significant. What we do today affects tomorrow. The way we spend our life now will have repercussions in eternity. To be good stewards of the fragile years we have been given will count forever.

The Watts hymn is sobering, but its message is positive. In fact, it is a prayer. It speaks so memorably, we use it at funerals and other difficult moments in life:

> *O God, our help in ages past,*
> *our hope for years to come,*
> *be thou our guide while life shall last,*
> *and our eternal home.*

Again, the scriptural original is poignant: "Lord, you have been our dwelling place throughout all generations" (Psalm 90:1); and the conclusion: "May the favor of the Lord our God rest upon us" (Psalm 90:17).

In stark contrast to the message of the psalm, a very different philosophy of history can be heard in our current environment. It is worth comparing to the biblical approach.

The current philosophy is basically a tragic view. Though we can sometimes carve out small pockets of meaning, overall there are no answers. No amount of moral uplift or words of hope can overcome the cold, hard fact of suffering. We may pray. We may look up to heaven. But heaven is empty. One might expect such a view to emerge from Europe and other parts of the world that have known cultural exhaustion. And it has. But it is increasingly heard in optimistic America. Something began to happen in the 1960s to cause a drift toward the darker view.

A gunshot. The man in the open limousine collapsed, his head covered with blood. Jacqueline Kennedy looked over and uttered two words: "No, no!"

The parallel world of horrors had intruded. America's youngest president had just been shot by a sniper from a warehouse window in Dallas. Hundreds of days and thousands of pages later, we were still looking desperately for a narrative that would make sense of this. Not that we didn't know the killer's name and some of the strange circumstances that made the shooting possible. But we needed to know more. Who was Lee Harvey Oswald? After the most exhaustive and heavily funded investigation in history, it seems certain that he was nothing more than a lonely, desperate man. No proven connections to the Mafia, no international conspiracy, no links to Kennedy's less-than-virtuous personal life. A conclusion altogether unworthy of the tragedy that shook the world. We need better answers.

Many of us remember exactly where we were on November 22, 1963. I was playing a soccer match for my college, the last game in the season, against the archrival. We had traveled down to Connecticut for a long weekend of sports and parties. Our team won the game, but strangely the crowd expressed no feeling, that we could tell. It was subdued.

In the second half of the game a rumor had spread that the president had been shot. The word had gone around like an echo in a canyon. When the game was over, it was more than a rumor. By the evening, as more details became known, what would have been a festive gathering ended as a brooding rumor mill. Was he really dead? Who could have done this? Was there some conspiracy at hand? Were we in some kind of danger? Were we at war?

My generation grew up very fast on that day. It was indeed the beginning of a most chaotic decade. Many of us felt a sort of disillusionment with the optimism of our parents. The hopeful atmosphere of the years following the greatest war in history, World War II, was replaced by a mixture of doubt, crazy idealism, hedonistic escape, and the quest for answers. We had questions our parents did not seem to understand. Someone quipped that we would never laugh again. To which the reply came, certainly we will laugh again, but we will never be young again.

Of course, outside America many had lost their youth long ago. Europeans, among others, had come into the age well fatigued from centuries of trouble on their own lands. Still, looking to America, some had dared hope that things could be different. It was not easy to see such a bright-eyed people, with its youthful president, so deeply shaken.

The great question on our minds could not be relieved by theories about growing up. We needed to know not about how the calamity would force Americans to come of age, but why it happened at all. Was it just an accident? Was it judgment? Had America grown arrogant in its new position "at the summit of the world," as Winston Churchill had put it just after the war? If this was God's judgment, then why did he not judge other things that were wrong with America? And why judge the whole country by the death of one man, albeit the president? Jacqueline Kennedy's "No, no!" told it like it was. We felt violated, outraged, incredulous. We knew something was terribly wrong.

Years later, after a number of other high-profile assassinations and a sobering failure in the Vietnam War, truistic explanations were running out. The mood turned to a darker, stoical posture. For many people, though by no means everyone, the absence of hope has become a sort of virtue. Better to be articulate about meaninglessness than to give false hope. Or any hope at all. Certainly this is not everyone's philosophy. But we are increasingly weary of plausible answers.

Whatever else may be represented by an emerging postmodern culture, the refusal of "grand narratives" is a constant. The present climate increasingly doubts that any bigpicture worldview has answers for the problem of evil. Universal standards, judgments based on absolutes, grand systems of meaning, are less and less plausible to the postmodern mindset.

LOOK UPON ME

Mark Slouka, an American writer known for his powerful short stories, recently spoke for this tragic point of view in a special millennial issue of *Harper's*. The title was "Blood on the Tracks." The subtitle asked the question, "Does senseless death reveal God, or His absence?"[1]

The piece describes a shift in the way we hear about bad news. Evil has always existed, but now, Slouka argues, the ability of the media to bring it into immediacy provokes "a need, a hunger, that cannot be satisfied, an existential dilemma fully worthy of Kafka." It's a theological issue, he admits. "Daily, our media drag us to God, force us to inquire after His meaning, then rub our noses in His absence."

Slouka recounts the horrible story of a mother and her four children being killed by a rapid train in the middle of the night in New England. Investigators desperately tried to reconstruct the events, but nothing in the facts came remotely close to explaining this senseless accident. The family had been in a shelter and was traveling at night, on foot, seeking a place to begin again. No drugs, no abuse, just an immigrant family's courageous determination to go somewhere else and make a new start. At one point they had to cross the railroad tracks.

"There was no narrative here, no saving plot." Slouka writes, "We'd been given a deconstructed poem." In the past, this kind of event would have made sense to Christians. But their theology is desperately unappealing. For example, he indicts Jonathan Edwards for preaching a God of pure vengeance. This God rubs our nose in the absence of meaning. He stretches the bow and aims the arrow at our hearts.

Slouka is glad to be rid of the kind of God who would orchestrate tragedies. But then the only thing left is, well, nothing: "There's blood on the tracks. A mother and four sons have died in Connecticut. Reflexively, we reach for the myth. But we've forgotten how to read. And we've forgotten how to believe. And the text has gone dark. And the author, whoever he was, if he was, has left."

The railroad metaphor turns on itself. History is going nowhere.

There is something darkly attractive about the stoical approach. It carries a sort of courageous realism. No nonsense. No leap of faith. Honesty. But is it honest, really? Is the absence of a narrative or saving plot not just as much a choice as the acceptance of the dreaded God of Jonathan Edwards? Is the deconstructed poem not finally based on as much faith, obstinate faith, as the despised theology Christians profess?

And there is serious distortion in Slouka's comparison. A careful reading of Jonathan Edwards reveals a very different picture from what we were told. Yes, his is a God of judgment. But there is far more to the story. The justice is deserved. Not individually by each family looking for a new beginning. Not always in ways that we can fully understand. We don't have the big picture. Why exactly did our young president have to be shot in Dallas on a day in the fall? We don't know altogether, but there are reasons, and God never acts arbitrarily. He doesn't play around with people. There is a "grand narrative."

Edwards's God is also a God of mercy. We do feel his absence, but that is what we should expect. If he seems to "rub our noses in his absence," it is because we have moved away, and doing so hurts. Somehow, Slouka misses the clear fact that the bow in Edwards's text is stretched, and the arrow is released, not against we who deserve it, but against God's only Son. It pierces Jesus' heart. Besides, the Lord daily confronts us with his presence. A severe presence at times, to be sure. He is not the God portrayed by the Hallmark card company. He is a God who gives meaning to a fallen world, to a creation gone wrong. A God who is not far from each one of us. A God who offers victory over oppression in the gospel. A God who will one day make secrets known and bring full justice to the oppressed, but also complete forgiveness to sinners.

The thesis of tragic realism has an air of nobility about it. It appears willing to accept adversity, to look death square in the face, and bravely admit it will consume us. The slow train of stoicism is coming but has no meaning. Instead, it leaves blood on the tracks. The contrast with the biblical picture is the more poignant in that there are some parallels.

Psalm 90, quoted earlier, has elements of sober realism in it. Echoing other parts of Scripture, the author reminds us that God does turn us back to dust. We are as the grass. Johannes Brahms powerfully set this idea to music in the *German Requiem*. With obdurate determination, the dirge-like kettledrums drive the chorus on, singing, "Behold, all flesh is grass, and all the beauty of man is like the flowers of the field" (from Isaiah 40:6). But the parallels end here. This is no deconstructed poem. There is a reason for our fragile natures.

It's a narrative of God's good creation gone bad. We are consumed because we have constructed a world without him—
or, worse, with him to blame. And this is really unlivable.

Yet God gives us relief. He provides meaning and hope.
Brahms's *Requiem* goes on to ask the Lord to "teach me my
life's end and how fleeting is my life." And it proclaims hope:
"Look upon me: for a while you have tribulation and toil, but
now you have great comfort." It's the pattern of the Psalms.
It's the story of redemption.

Stoic pessimism is many things, but it is not innocent.
Slouka is not an objective journalist. He is angry, yes, angry
with God! His disposition makes him oblivious to the nu-
ances of justice. He is unable to see that the books are not yet
balanced, and that if they were, all of us would fall short. Nor
can he know about severe mercy, the mercy that gives grace,
provisionally today, fully tomorrow. The disposition of anger
turns the lack of detailed answers into a dilemma, rather than
a mystery.

The absence of full disclosure is actually a good sign. It's
a condition of a truly transcendent God. Evil is not arbitrary.
Though so much is indeed mysterious to us, yet ultimately
there is purpose even in affliction, because God is there, inef-
fable but fair, inscrutable but merciful. If we think God
should not allow evil, it may be that our image of God has little to do with the Lord who reigns, robed in majesty, armed
with strength (Psalm 93). Wanting to separate God from evil
stems from good intentions. But it confuses the good with
the benign. It confuses all suffering with cruelty, forgetting
that justice can also hurt, even if it is good.

Dylan's song continues, "But the enemy I see wears a
cloak of decency. . . ." On the surface it seems very decent to
protect God from the charge of evil. We are happier thinking

of him as a kindly grandfather in the sky. But the price to pay is dear. Such thinking makes the presence of evil inexplicable. It offers a cloak of decency, but not the truth. Better to have the slow, slow train coming up around the bend.

So, where do you stand in all this? Are you angry with God? Have you demanded—and abandoned hope for—an explanation, never considering that the explanation is larger, fuller, than you could comprehend? Do you prefer the stoic posture of self-sufficiency, or the honest question, "Why, O Lord," followed by the mysterious yet reassuring answer, "Let God be God; he understands"?

NINE 🖋

GOD AND EVIL

If indeed we must let God be God, is there anything we can do? Do we throw up our hands and await the world to come? Or can we be engaged in the fight against evil?

THE WHOLE SCHEME OF THINGS

Albert Camus (1913–60) is less influential today than he once was, though every so often he makes a comeback. Recently some notes for what would have been another novel of his, *The First Man*, were published, and that brought his memory into the light. From the title alone, one can tell how captivated he was by biblical themes. Many of his other writings have similar mythical or theological themes: *The Myth of Sisyphus*, *The Righteous*, *The Rebel*, *The Fall*, etc.

Camus was born in Algeria, and his North African roots were never far from him, even when he moved to Paris and became a world figure. He won the Nobel Prize for literature in 1957. Though he did not care for the label, he was called an Existentialist and was compared and contrasted with the other great French philosopher of the twentieth century, Jean-Paul Sartre.

Camus began his philosophical itinerary with a strong dose of pessimism. By the year 1943 he had concluded that the most plausible myth, or explanation for the world, was that it was absurd. Not that one should ever give in to absurdity; though the myth gave us no true, foundational reason for existence, one should never live by it. His most popular novel is *The Stranger*. It centers on a sort of antihero, Meursault, who moves along in life without any overall purpose or guiding ethic. He shoots a man for no reason, and then dies in prison after long and unfruitful discussions with a priest.

These were the war years in France. Camus moved to Saint Etienne, and then to a tiny village in the Ardèche plateau, called Le Chambon-sur-Lignon. There he set up in a small apartment and completed a manuscript for a longer novel, first called *Exiles in the Plague*, and then simply *The Plague*.

Set in Algeria, it is the story of the bubonic plague spreading throughout the port city of Oran. Though a self-contained tale, it is clearly also an allegory for the evils of the Third Reich. The plague represents the Nazi hegemony. The rats are the Germans. Two hundred thousand citizens of Oran are captured by the plague. Two hundred million Europeans were in effect prisoners of the Nazis. Rations, denouncements, the black market—all these features of life in a pandemic are echoes of life in occupied France. The healthy are indifferent, except for a few who are working hard toward stemming the disease. The French were, on the whole, oblivious to the horrors of the concentration camps.

Camus's novel is clearly about a subject even deeper than the Nazi occupation. It is about the problem of evil. His philosophy emerges in the story. He had developed his view of the absurd and now was trying to overcome it. What he saw around him caused him to abandon the idea of absurdity, which was too comfortable, and not particularly hopeful. He was now confronted with horror, not absurdity. Because the plague is horrible, not absurd, the only proper tactic toward it is to rebel.

Rebellion against evil is a constant theme for Camus. He works out the reasons for it in this powerful novel, one that marked a generation. Much of the intrigue takes place in the conversations held by each character. Two of them are central. Through their utterances Camus shows forth his tremendous knowledge of the great thinkers, both ancient and modern, both believing and unbelieving—thinkers who have wrestled with the problem of good and evil. The two central characters are Dr. Rieux, the dedicated physician, a reluctant atheist who tirelessly treats the victims of the plague, and Father Paneloux, a priest who broadly represents the theological commitments of Saint Augustine. Rieux, more than anyone, is Camus's mouthpiece. Still, he has sympathies with Paneloux as well, though he finds him inconsistent and naïve.

At one point in the story Dr. Rieux is speaking with his young friend Tarrou. Tarrou is trying to understand how a doctor could work so hard to reverse the plague when he did not believe in any larger scheme of things. He asks him, "Why do you yourself show such devotion, considering you don't believe in God?" The doctor promptly answers, "Nobody can, even Paneloux, or they would do nothing."

What is he saying? The idea is that if you believe in God, you let him do all the work. If God were good, and powerful, he would not allow the plague and other horrors to occur. Since he isn't doing anything, he must not exist. Even the priest has to wonder about the absence of God.

Rieux is a sensitive man, who originally entered his medical profession "abstractly," as he put it, without a deeper sense of vocation, but then got caught up with the urgency of the situation. The healing arts were his way to fight against evil. He was "outraged by the whole scheme of things," he told his young friend. A revealing statement—no separation between good and evil, between God and creation, or between the original creation and the fall. He was outraged by them all.

Camus further narrates that the doctor "believed himself to be on the right road—in fighting against *creation as he found it*." Later, he says that humanity is basically good, but has merely given way to ignorance. After ignorance is compounded, it can lead to the horrors of totalitarian domination. The only thing at fault is "creation"—that is, the whole world, except people.

IT'S NO ILLUSION

Camus's philosophy, and that of thousands like him, is that evil cannot be explained. It can only be opposed. If God were all-powerful and good at the same time, there would be no evil. Despite all claims to the contrary, this is fundamentally a position of despair. If the problem is in the creation—that is, the way things are—then basically there can be no hope. How can we change what we are? How can we improve if we are only the product of the environment? We may admire Camus for his integrity and his courage. Indeed he did a great deal in his life to oppose evil as he found it. But fighting the creation is ultimately hopeless.

Camus's philosophy has this going for it: He believed evil to be real. Many do not. There are large families of Asian religions that consider evil to be illusory.

In classical Hinduism, evil is considered *maya*, a Sanskrit term meaning "distance from the center." The idea is that the universe centers in the Brahman, where all of reality is concentrated. As you move toward the periphery, you encounter the less solid, the less eternal. At the edge, you have the ephemeral. Suffering, disease, sin, death itself—these are near the outer edge, far, far from the Brahman.

Buddhism, something of a reform movement within Hinduism, makes this even more practical. Following the teachings of Siddartha, it developed various disciplines by which one can get rid of the illusion of evil. Exercises and meditation techniques help adherents take all of the human emotions less seriously, until one attains the state of Nirvana, complete release from this world and its cares.

Western versions of evil-as-illusion abound. Early in the history of the church, Augustine offered a partial answer, but it was fundamentally insufficient. He held that evil was simply the dark side, the *contra boni*. The good is real. Evil is a pale shadow that only makes sense by contrast to the good. This view was an advance over the popular idea at the time of evil as a powerful force, nearly equal to God. It relativized evil, making it something negative, without substance, which notion has a grain of truth in it. But Augustine borrowed too heavily from Plato and his theory of ideas and shadows.

At a far less thoughtful level, many self-help theories and stiff-upper-lip moralistic views tell us that no problem is so important that it cannot be overcome with a little effort "Don't let it get you down," we hear, in many versions. There is a Christian version that blithely says when, for example, someone dies, "It's a blessing," or parrots the Bible verse unsympathetically, "All things work together for good."

Evil is no illusion. Camus had it right. Try explaining to an

Indian mother whose child died in infancy that it is *maya*. Try telling the family of a Holocaust victim that all things work together for good, without painting a much, much larger picture. Evil is all too real. It has penetrated every realm of life.

Indeed, the greater problem for most of us is not accepting the reality of evil, but understanding how evil could be at all. Especially certain forms of it. The twentieth century was the setting for the most unspeakable crimes, the most unthinkable evil ever seen. No amount of millennial fever could atone for the immediate past. We cannot here present a litany of those abominations. But neither may we simply pass over the twin infamies of Communism and National Socialism (Nazism), which brought expropriation, deportation, and genocide to unheard-of levels. Indeed, the mention of these is often enough to discourage many from considering a God who claims to be good and all-powerful.

The Bible offers no simple explanation for evil. Indeed, no acceptable, logical explanation for it is ever given. Yet neither does the Bible mystify evil so that it becomes incomprehensible. This is as we should expect, since the fundamental character of evil is this: to be against God. This makes it, as Karl Barth once put it, "the impossible possibility." The reason for its power, its horror, is that being against God, who is good, is heinous by definition. It is the very essence of disgrace. So intense, so ignominious are certain examples of evil that the demonic must be evoked. To be sure, evil comes at the suggestion of the devil, a beautiful angel gone wrong. But it is received and decided by men and women.

Because evil now characterizes human affairs, it has a character; it takes on certain contours. The basic form, at the heart of it, is the attempt to construct a world purely of human wisdom, a world where God is superfluous. To accomplish this, two simultaneous moves are necessary. First, outright ways to deny God and the biblical interpretation of his world must be found. Second, a fair amount of duplication, or counterfeit, is needed for it to qualify as evil.

Consider (much too briefly) the twin evils of Communism and National Socialism. There are important differences between them, of course. Communism is a more "optimistic" ideology, believing in radical justice and equality. Nazism is "pessimistic," demanding that we get rid of the illusion of peace and justice, and look for deserving power instead. Communism works through education; Nazism works through resentment. Yet there is also something in common. They share what we just characterized as the essence of evil.

Both respond to the biblical roots of Western culture by denying and imitating them at the same time. In both scenarios, a program or "plan" (that's the exact term) begins by eradicating the biblical soul that characterizes Western civilization. Then it goes on to reproduce fundamental features of that same biblical soul, albeit in counterfeit form. That is how evil always operates.

More specifically, what is outrightly denied in Communism? Communism resents the implied negative judgment so often proclaimed in the Scriptures. For example, the Ten Commandments set a standard that no one can keep. They clearly are statements of our inability to help ourselves as human beings, at least by our own resources. By denying that verdict at the outset, Communism denies our resulting need for grace centered in Christ.

The step of counterfeiting must follow. The Bolshevik ideology stated that a "new man" would emerge when the plan would be implemented. Careful programing, political transformation, revolution, education, and re-education would lead the way. Various measures of coercion were needed when reason alone did not yield the Communist vision. The Gulag prison system provided an important safeguard against dissent. When this proved too slow, purges through mass starvation became necessary.

In this way Communism counterfeits the message of the Old Testament, with its prophets and the Exodus. Peace, justice, equality—these biblical values are predicted, secularized, and then forced into play by cruel compulsion rather than spiritual redemption. Perhaps one of the reasons this grand leftist scheme has been so attractive all over the world is its distant echo of biblical eschatology (the doctrine of the last things). But the spiritual dynamic necessary for peace, justice, and equality is missing, having been replaced by tyrannical force.

National Socialism denies the Old Testament altogether, charging that the Old Testament soul actually poisoned modern civilization. The only solution is a return to the prebiblical days of pure-blooded paganism, where heroes and the *Volk* roamed the earth. Hitler declared Jews to be literally inhuman, not children of the same God who created the rest of humanity. By expunging the Jews and other non-Aryans, a secular kingdom, the Reich, could be ushered in. The counterfeiting of an elect, chosen people thus justifies any conceivable measure to hasten the coming of the true kingdom— even the unspeakable death camps.

With this admittedly oversimplified description we still have not "explained" evil. It is in one way inexplicable. Why would humanity want to take the blessed world of God's good creation and betray its Creator? Why would an entire people as gifted as the Russians or the Germans participate in an ideology that justifies cruelty beyond measure? Is it only a particular people, or do we all somehow participate in cosmic treason?

All of us do this. Evil is not only a program sponsored by the Communists or the Nazis. It is our common desire, our inclination. To describe it this way is not to explain it, but it is to contain it. It is contained because it is not a final mystery, but centers on human responsibility. Otherwise there is no hope. No guilt, no atonement.

TRUE GUILT AND TRUE HOPE

Here is the hard part. Unless we can see our guilt for what it is, then no real hope is available. When I first came into contact with living Christian faith, this was the most difficult thing for me to accept. I could believe the religion is true, and I was convinced of the claims of Jesus Christ and of the Bible's authority. But I could not accept the idea that I personally was guilty enough to merit God's eternal displeasure. The idea of hell seemed disproportionate with the various sins I reckoned I had committed. Stalin and Hitler, yes, they deserved the worst. But most of us are not monsters, nor can we conceive falling into such depravity as they.

For a while I was content to let the tradition of the church judge this for me, but without feeling it, without its making an impact on my soul. That judgment is clear, of course. The uniform tradition of the church, springing from abundant biblical teaching, is patent:

> We believe that man was created pure and perfect in the image of God, and that by his own guilt he fell from the grace which he received, and is thus alienated from God,

the fountain of justice and all good, so that his nature is totally corrupt. (Confession of La Rochelle, Art. 10)

Not words one will find in the therapeutic language of modern pop psychology!

It was only gradually, walking with the Lord, having him shine his probing, often intrusive, light on me, that I began to realize that the doctrine applies to me. Many things contributed to my reality check. One was trying hard to be strong in some moral area, and failing over and over again. Another was the test of honesty: if I knew no one, not even God, were looking, would I do this? I became more aware of motives. Mine were often less than noble.

And then different awakenings drove home the awful truth that I was a sinner. Thinking myself free from racism, I found myself participating in racist institutional structures without opposing them. Thinking myself generous, I found myself willing to give to others only to a point, usually not to the point of personal loss or sacrifice. Thinking myself unboundedly grateful to God, I found myself poor and awkward in praise and thanksgiving.

The story of Aleksandr Solzhenitsyn has often been told. His voice in declaring to the world the dreadful reality of life behind the Iron Curtain was the loudest and most eloquent. *The Gulag Archipelago* is a three-volume exposé of the awful truth about Communism from someone who once believed it. In it he describes his conversion to the gospel.

He was in prison, accused of criticizing Stalin. There he met Dr. Boris Kornfeld, a Jew who had become a follower of Jesus Christ. One night, Kornfeld was setting forth the idea of guilt to him. Suffering in this life is always deserved, he explained, and whether the transgression was committed by commission or omission, it would ultimately be disclosed. That night the doctor was murdered by the prison guards for no apparent reason. Solzhenitsyn was deeply troubled. He had lost a friend and a mentor.

But he had not lost the teaching proffered by his fellow prisoner. He began to think about what Dr. Kornfeld had told him. How does a human being become evil, he wondered? Then he realized, he was no better than the guards. In his youth he had thought himself superior to everyone else. He had thought himself to be infallible. This was in fact cruelty, he reckoned, because it was a surge of power, undeserved power. What he attributed to the good was actually evil. Upon further reflection, Solzhenitsyn realized evil is not so much in political struggles, nor in class conflicts, but in the human heart. Guilty, yes, but now liberated, because he knew the truth.

But, we still may want to ask, Where is God in all this? Perhaps the guilt is mine, but how could God allow a world of guilt and evil to come into existence?

Here we come close to an unanswerable question. We can only plead for the avoidance of two equally wrong notions. The first is that God is not in control. This has been an attractive option for many thinkers. Evil exists because God is somehow less than powerful. It may be theorized that he gave up some of his power to give us free choice. Or, as some say, he is somehow absent, distant from the world of human affairs, and when it comes to the problem of evil, even God does not fully comprehend it.

Consider what is lost with this view. First, and most crucial, God is lost in the balance. If God is less than all-powerful, if the Creator is less than the governor of all things, can we name him God? Second, evil itself is not possible without

God's sovereignty. He makes our choices valid, he ensures that evil is real and not an illusion, not despite his power, but because of it. That was W. H. Auden's discovery after the Yorkville cinema experience. There had to be a force big enough to explain Hitler. We may not particularly like this idea, because it means God is somehow the one who puts evil into his plan. But if he is God, how could it be otherwise?

The second error to avoid is that God is in control, all right, and is responsible for evil at the same time. Put another way, God would be the author of sin. If this is true, then all is lost, for such a God is no longer remotely good, and therefore he is something else than God. Furthermore, the human situation would be hopeless since we are neither responsible nor guilty, and thus we have no moral leverage.

So where does this leave us? With a mystery, in one sense. How can God be in control yet not responsible? Again, though, this is the conviction of the church, as it interprets Scripture. It has perhaps never been better expressed than in the Westminster Confession of Faith:

> God from all eternity did, by the most wise and holy counsel of his own will, freely and unchangeably ordain whatsoever comes to pass: yet so, as thereby neither is God the author of sin, nor is violence offered to the will of the creatures, nor is the liberty or contingency of second causes taken away, but rather established. (3.1)

The mystery comes at the colon. God is utterly in control, to the point that he ordains everything. This must include the existence and role of evil in the world. So he ordains evil. Yet (a powerful connective, if there ever was one), so that somehow he is not morally guilty for evil. In fact, the integrity and meaning of human will, as well as the reality of everything else ("second causes"), far from being denied, is somehow upheld, determined—everything that is opposite of "illusion."

GOD AND HUMANITY AGAINST EVIL

The supreme irony of Camus's *The Plague* is that it was written in *Le Chambon* during the Second World War. This happens to be the village where over five thousand Jews, many of them children, were hidden from the Nazis. The villagers were mostly Protestants, *Huguenots*, as they were known. They were sensitive to religious persecution, having known it themselves in generations past. They were also proud to be spiritual descendants of Israel, people of the Book.

The most astonishing aspect of their sacrifice and courage is how unheroic they considered themselves to be. When asked years later by one of the survivors why they had done it, the answer was, "Well, wouldn't you?" And then, when he probed further, they would say, "God says to love him, and love your neighbor; what we did is normal."

Camus knew this was going on. But in *The Plague* he does not seem to have made the connection. The people who really give of themselves sacrificially are not the Dr. Rieux of this world, but the biblically directed followers of Jesus Christ.

There is an episode in the gospel of John that has always moved me. Chapter 11 is the report of Lazarus, who died and then was raised from the dead by Jesus. The passage reveals something of the emotional life of our Lord.[1] Jesus was quite attached to Lazarus's family. Several times the text tells us of his love for him and his two sisters. When this man died, Martha came to Jesus and, scolding him, suggested, "Lord, if you had been here, my brother would not have died" (verse 21).

How often has this thought been expressed by suffering people: *Lord, if you had been here . . . ?* But Jesus gave her an eschatological answer: "Your brother will rise again" (verse 23). Martha knew about the final resurrection of the dead. But Jesus refocused her doctrine: "I am the resurrection and the life. He who believes in me will live, even though he dies" (verse 25). Martha did believe and made the same confession of faith as Peter had done earlier: "I believe that you are the Christ" (verse 27).

Then comes the compelling part. Martha's sister Mary came to Jesus with the same admonition. "Lord, if you had been here, my brother would not have died," she was weeping (verses 32–33; the original word means "wailing"). This time Jesus was overcome. The translation has it that he was "deeply moved in spirit and troubled" (verses 33). The expression is repeated (verse 38). The Greek verb, *embrimaomai*, has a far stronger sense than is rendered by "to groan" (KJV). It means "to be furious." Literally it refers to the horse snorting with rage. Jesus, who is the resurrection, was enraged at the evil of death. Warfield puts it eloquently:

> *The spectacle of the distress of Mary and her companions enraged Jesus because it brought poignantly home to his consciousness the evil of death, its unnaturalness, its "violent tyranny" as Calvin (on verse 38) phrases it. In Mary's grief, he "contemplates"—still to adopt Calvin's words (on verse 33),—"the general misery of the whole human race" and burns with rage against the oppressor of men.[2]*

Jesus' tears are significant. But so also is his wrath. He is not only the redeemer, the *I am* of resurrection power, but he is the lover of our souls, the furiously compassionate Savior. He raised Lazarus from the dead then and there. He called him out of the grave. He could only do this because, driven by his rage at evil, he would head unflinchingly toward Jerusalem, then to his own grave after a scandalous death on a Roman gibbet.

But the most significant thing about this episode for our discussion is that he could be enraged against sin, without for a moment putting into question the sovereignty of God. Neither did he question the Father's place as Creator, nor his own place as the mediator of all creation. This was the very opposite of Rieux's fighting "the creation as he found it." In the biblical view, one may, and must, fight evil without fighting God. That is because in the fight, God is on the side of the good, stopping at nothing to overcome the evil in its way.

This is the key to social reform. It is thought by many that Christianity is repressive, leads to war, is against women, and is the opiate of the people. Granted, many mistakes have been made. But the truth is, the gospel has been one of the principal agents for the liberation of victim groups and minorities. But it has done so with love, not by revolution. It has sought to do so on God's terms, not according to a secular human-rights scheme.

Where do we stand on these issues? Are we willing to enact reform God's way? A friend of mine likes to say, Christ is not a means to our goals. He sets new goals for us altogether. It's better that way.

TEN 🖋

YES, EXIT!

A re all religions the same? Are they basically different
means to a common end? Will all of them give power,
power for change? Or is there something unique about the
Christian faith?

COMING THROUGH FOR ME

It was a hot, rainy day in Taipei. And noisy. The streets
were full of people, cars, and motorbikes. Markets everywhere
were selling food, clothing—products of all kinds. In Taipei
one cannot walk more than a few blocks without seeing a temple. Most are small, but a few are large and imposing. That day
we entered one of the largest temples in the country.

Hsing Tien was alive with worshipers, visitors, monks,
guides, young and old, rich and poor. Its graceful, intertwin-
ing arches drew our eyes from the busy crowd in the court-
yard upwards to the sky. Bright colors—reds, gold, pastels—
dazzled the senses. There was sound everywhere: flutes
wailing; drums beating; groups chanting, shouting, moaning;

and conversations everywhere. Not that chaos reigned. The Taiwanese people are most orderly and respectful despite the swarming crowds.

The themes of *Hsing Tien* are a mixture of ancient religion and modern tradition. The announced goal in the pamphlet we were given was to "conduct secular achievement out of celestial emanation." Presumably a translation from Mandarin, the phrase was explained by the guides and the pamphlets. The temple is a place of purification, from which worshipers can go out to the larger world in a spirit of peace. The hardships and sufferings of all who enter and contribute then become a sort of model of atonement to the benefit of participants. Thus the gods bless those who enter.

The religion is syncretistic. Five principal gods are worshiped, including *Hsing Tien*. And the "holy spirits" of the three principal Chinese religions—Confucian, Buddhist, and Taoist—are included in the pantheon. The gods are all descendants of the Supreme God of Heaven (*En Chu Kong*).

The temple has several social objectives. One is ethical instruction. Good moral conduct is considered the "best offering to god," far better than material objects. Indeed, offerings of things are discouraged, though we saw many people bringing them anyway. General education is also a priority. The temple has a large library full of resources and references on all subjects, including children's books, newspapers, and textbooks. Then there are considerable medical and charitable works, which include a hospital, scholarship funds, and rescue missions.

Most people we saw came looking for a combination of these loftier things and things very down-to-earth. In one place, a good number were lining up to receive an incense-waving by the qualified healer. Lighted sticks were dispensing waves of incense onto objects or people. One could ask for a piece of clothing to be steeped in the vapor, in hope that the magic would work on the person wearing it. One could present a document, perhaps a legal paper served, hoping for a clear resolution of whatever dispute was involved. One could ask for an incense-wave onto some part of the body for protection or healing.

In another place a large group was gathered to give alms and to ask the gods to make sure their children took care of their memory after death. This would be the guarantee of happiness in the world beyond. In yet another place, people were gathered around an enormous statue, placing gifts by the feet and singing songs of praise. The statue represented a hero who had been slain as he protected one of the gods. They asked for courage to be like him.

As we gazed at this amazing scene, a guide came over to speak with us. She was most pleasant and was anxious for us to understand some of the dynamics of the temple. Not far into the conversation, she asked if we were Christians. When we confirmed her guess, she told us something about her own spiritual journey.

She was raised in a Christian home. But the God of the Bible never came through for her, she explained. She had prayed for many benefits, some concrete, such as money, promotion at work, more children. She never felt anything or saw any proof that this God was at work. Then she changed over to Taoism, or at least a folk religion with a Taoist character. The answers began to come, in abundance, she averred. Her philosophy was simple, she went on. Your God is far removed, too far above the world to care. The gods of the temple are alive and well, and they give evident satisfaction for all your requests.

Not an easy position to dispute. On the surface, it was quite like the story of the blind man in John's gospel, mentioned earlier. Our friend went where the proof, the measurable evidence, could be found. It would have been a mistake, at least at first, to dispute the evidence. Our Western tendency, informed as it is by secularism, was to be skeptical about such answers to prayer as she mentioned. How could she be sure, we might have asked, that getting a promotion at work was because of the benevolence of one of the temple gods? And how could she explain the occasional lack of answers, or even contrary answers?

This would likely have been a futile discussion. What we began to answer instead—before being cut short by time constraints—was that her requests, while understandable, were misguided. What she was asking for, in effect, was security here on earth. She measured it partly by such things as money, children, and other visible tokens, and partly by signs of moral improvement. But her needs were far deeper. She needed to be secure in a far greater arena than this world or even the world to come. She needed, as everyone in the world does, to be secure with God. She needed to know that her guilt could be removed and that God himself would henceforth be the light upon her path, even become her friend.

But how do you explain this in a way that does not sound uncaring? How do you explain that these other things she was longing for do matter—they matter to God—but not first and foremost?

Jesus explained the same principle to his disciples, in a pastoral vein: "Therefore I tell you, do not worry about your life, what you will eat or drink; or about your body, what you will wear. Is not life more important than food, and the body more important than clothes?" (Matthew 6:25). He went on to say, "For the pagans run after these things, and your heavenly Father knows that you need them." And then, he enjoined, "Seek first his kingdom and his righteousness, and all these things will be given to you as well" (verses 32–33).

How can we understand that though our earthly needs may be great indeed, there is something even more important? How can we see that however desperate our sufferings may be here on earth, our first calling is to know God, and to be known by him?

Jesus' diagnosis of the world religions is severe. The word translated "pagan" is more neutral in the Greek. It is *ethnē*, from which we get our word "ethnic." Here it means "peoples" or even "nations," in the sense of the non-Jews. The ethnic groups outside of the covenant "run after all these things"; that is, they look frantically to find security from suffering and want. The Father knows we all need these things. He is not oblivious to them, or faraway, as our dear guide had imagined. But he wants for us to have much more. He wants us to have life itself. He wants us to be in his kingdom, to be ruled and guided by no less a Lord than himself. He wants us to be clothed first with his righteousness, a righteousness that endures, and only then with physical raiment.

When tempted, Jesus refused to turn stones into bread. Even food, good as it is, cannot rival the surpassing value of the Word of God: "Man does not live on bread alone, but on every word that comes from the mouth of God" (Matthew 4:4). How could he say this? How could the one who directed his church to feed the poor put a Word first? Because that Word is God's living source of food, the "bread of life." Knowing God, being alive in him, is even better than food.

YOU TAUGHT HIM TO
TRUST IN YOU

Paradoxically, being firmly established in God's kingdom actually prepares us for guidance in ways no ethnic religion can. God will in fact provide in all areas necessary for our existence. His way of doing that is not always the way we would script. But he does it in the perfect wisdom of his own timing.

Consider an episode in Augustine's *Confessions*, a work that ranks as one of the great spiritual masterpieces of literature. In his *Confessions* Augustine meditates on his life and mixes elements of autobiography with prayers and biblical commentary. He tells of his early life, his conversion to Christian faith, and some of his adventures as a believer living in the fifth century.

In one place he tells of his best friend, Alypius, who came from his hometown in Africa (*Confessions* 6.[esp. 7–9]). Augustine was Alypius's professor, and clearly the younger man was his favorite student. Both were former unbelievers, and they loved to endlessly discuss life and philosophy together.

Before his conversion, Alypius had a singular weakness: he "had lost his heart and his head to the games in the amphitheater." We know something about these games—violent, blood-thirsty spectacles, where gladiators fought animals and each other to the death, merely for entertainment. Augustine explains how he was used as the instrument, without knowing it, to prevent the young man from wasting his talents in "this thoughtless, impetuous enthusiasm for futile pastimes."

One day Alypius showed up at a lesson when it happened that his teacher was waxing on the subject of moral improvement. As if by chance, Augustine gave an illustration involving the arena. His words, though spoken as an aside, were used to cure Alypius, at least temporarily, of his habit:

> For after he had heard my words, Alypius hastened to drag himself out of the deep pitfall into which, dazzled by the allure of pleasure, he had plunged of his own accord. By a great effort of self-control he shook himself free of all the dirt of the arena and never went near it again.

Shortly thereafter, both men became converts to Christian faith. It was sweet fellowship, for their friendship was able to continue at an even deeper level than before since they shared in this newfound understanding. For a while, all was well. But then temptation came and Alypius's moral integrity was seriously threatened.

Though converted, Alypius had not entirely shaken the ethical system that had defined him for many years. Like Augustine, he had trusted in an ethic of self-control based on the influential religion known as "Manichaeism." According to this system, people were caught between good and evil, light and darkness, and they could move closer to the good by strong resolve and self-improvement tactics. Augustine says of his friend,

> He particularly admired the Manichees for their ostensible continence, which he thought quite genuine, though of course it was merely a nonsensical and deceitful method of trapping precious souls which had not learnt to feel the depth of real virtue. (6.7)

This is a pregnant statement. A great deal hangs in the balance.

What happened, then? The two men went to Rome. And there, Alypius had a terrible downfall. He got an "extraordinary craving for gladiatorial shows," and though he tried to resist, his friends managed to entice him. At first, he refused to go. But then he made a bargain: "You may drag me there bodily . . . but it will be just as if I were not present, I shall prove myself stronger than you or the games" (6.8). So he went to a game, but decided he could still withstand by closing his eyes. As Augustine said, though, "If only he had closed his ears as well!" He got right back into the blood and violence of the games.

The following description could be a modern psychological report on an addiction:

> An incident in the fight drew a great roar from the crowd, and this thrilled him so deeply that he could not contain his curiosity. Whatever caused the uproar, he was confident that, if he saw it, he would find it repulsive and remain master of himself. So he opened his eyes, and his soul was stabbed with a wound more deadly than any which the gladiator, whom he was so anxious to see, had received in his body. He fell, and fell more pitifully than the man whose fall had drawn that roar of excitement from the crowd. The din had pierced his ears and forced him to open his eyes, laying his soul open to receive the wound which struck it down. (6.8)

Augustine goes on to describe Alypius as "drunk with the fascination of bloodshed." He was "a fit companion for the friends who had brought him." His mind was "diseased."

How could this have happened? He was a Christian, but he had fallen hard. Would God abandon him? Was he beyond hope? With poignant realism, Augustine reflects prayerfully on the cause of his friend's predicament—his resolve to stand against evil on his own strength: "This was presumption, not courage. The weakness of his soul was in relying upon himself instead of trusting in you." (6.8) The cure was in the diagnosis. Alypius still had much to learn about trusting in God's power, not in the limited power of human virtue. Eventually he would, and a great victory would occur in his life.

This change came much later. Indeed, Alypius eventually became a bishop and preached the gospel far and wide. He administered the sacraments. His extraordinary skills were used to judge different church cases that came up. He demonstrated great wisdom.

What is the point of this story? Augustine is telling us that the system of ethics taught in ancient Greece—though lofty, noble, even admirable—could not give what we really need. Not only could it not give us that closeness to God—that righteousness of the kingdom that our Lord spoke about—but it could not even give strength to face the serious trials of life. Basically, Augustine is saying that if you think you are strong, be very careful. You may not know how weak you really are. Unless you know God and are known by him, you cannot endure the challenges, the hardships, the sufferings of this life, let alone find the peace and healing your soul desperately needs.

THE FAITHFUL GOD

The apostle Paul gives a similar teaching to his readers in Corinth. Though Christians, the people of this urban church were still counting on their status as proud Greeks to bring them through certain challenges. They were often more impressed with Greek culture and Roman ethics than with the gospel. They had apparently grasped the *freedom*, the privilege of the true knowledge of Christ, but were vulnerable because they had not connected that freedom to responsibility. Paul's approach with them is a combination of warning, exhortation, and elucidation. He warns them about the danger of spiritual pride. He exhorts them to be aware of the way God leads during trials. He elucidates the true meaning of freedom in the service of God.

"If you think you are standing firm, be careful that you don't fall!" Paul tells them (1 Corinthians 10:12). He illustrates his concern from the Old Testament, where God's people had fallen very hard during their sojourn in the desert. If that could happen to Israel, with all their privilege, then it could also happen to the Corinthians, despite their own privileges and gifts. They were counting far too much on their brilliance and their rich supply of spiritual gifts. These were gifts from God, but Paul wanted them to know that even these will not stand them in good stead when faced with certain trials. Like Alypius, the Corinthians were saying to themselves, in effect, *I can handle this, I'll just close my eyes.* They claimed their great spirituality would save them.

How does Paul handle the problem? He could have said, "Please be a little more *balanced.* In addition to your precious freedom, go back to the law!" But he does not do that at all. Rather, intriguingly, he builds on their very own premise. He says, in effect, "You are free because you are living in the end times [1 Corinthians 10:11]; your freedom is therefore great beyond measure. That freedom *will* stand you in good stead, provided you understand what it is about at a deeper level than you do. You need to know what real freedom is." He explains that everything is permissible, though not beneficial. Freedom is not license.

Paul also explains the reality of the trials the people of

Corinth would endure. Trials will come. That is the plight of end-of-times Christians. And the trials will be hard at times, harder than you imagine. But his main point to them as they face these trials is this: *"God is faithful"* (1 Corinthians 10:13).

This is the foundation. This is the presupposition that makes biblical ethics completely and radically different from the Greek and Roman system. It is an ethic of full dependence upon God. It looks well beyond the gifts, and to the Giver.

How does this work itself out in practice? Here the apostle is very down-to-earth. First, he reinforces the simple fact that trials will come. Physical trials, spiritual trials, they will occur because of our position as end-of-times believers in a fallen world. It is the common human condition. When it comes, then you should not think it unusual. You should not be caught off guard as though this were a total surprise. We are not alone. It happens to everyone.

> *No temptation has seized you except what is common to man. And God is faithful; he will not let you be tempted beyond what you can bear. But when you are tempted, he will also provide a way out so that you can stand up under it. (1 Corinthians 10:13)*

When my wife and I were a young married couple, we lived with an aged professor and his wife. She was from the Baltics, of Russian descent, and would often tell us extraordinary stories of her experiences in the earlier part of the twentieth century. She had fled during the invasions of the Red Army and met her husband in Germany. Now, living in Philadelphia, she nurtured her memories. She had suffered much, but had a deep trust in God's faithfulness. She told us once that during the birth of one of her children she had an extremely long labor. She came close to death. But in the midst of her intense pains, she suddenly remembered that women all over the world have gone through this kind of suffering. She was not alone. This thought brought her comfort.

We are not alone. Our sufferings are common to humanity, not because everyone has had the exact same level of experience, but because suffering is suffering. Every kind of suffering is shared by all of humankind. Some suffer physically, some spiritually. Some are persecuted; some are ill; some are oppressed. If you are a Christian, you will by many hardships enter the kingdom of God (Acts 14:22). Do you think to yourself, *No one has ever gone through this; I am alone in my suffering.* It is not true. God isn't singling you out.

Are you single and wish you were married? Is there no man for you? Has God forgotten you? No, he is faithful. Other singles are suffering the same feelings. Are you married, but unhappily? Is your spouse difficult? Has God forgotten you? No, he is faithful. Don't go by appearances; everyone has suffered.

But there is more. Paul tells his readers that even their trials are sent by God! How can this be? Why would God actually orchestrate a hardship into the life of his children? We cannot know all the reasons. It is often not appropriate to try and explain. One reason, though, is that God is so anxious to have us for himself, to free us from our dependencies, that he often removes the props. He may use harsh measures to drive the point home, but it is a point worth enduring. Yet the premise is always the foundation: God is faithful. He never plays around with people. He only allows hardship when it is for the good (Romans 8:28).

Indeed, this faithful God will never let his children suffer beyond what they can endure (1 Corinthians 10:13). We may think he does. We may imagine the situation is unbearable. But it is not. Why would he allow that? No hardship is too difficult, because with each hardship, there is a way of escape.

There is a powerful play written by Jean-Paul Sartre called, in English, *No Exit*. The original is *Huis Clos*, which means "behind closed doors." The play is about three characters who know too much about each other and so are co-dependent. They dare not leave the room for fear that one of the others will denounce them. Thus while physically free to come and go, they are morally captive. The statement is made at one point, "Hell is other people." The play is dark beyond measure. A number of the actors who were its earliest interpreters actually committed suicide.

If, indeed, there is no God, as Sartre thought, then hell is other people. It is hopeless. But if, as it is, God is there and he is faithful, then hell is not other people. It's living without him. It is being alive but dead to his grace. Eternal death is hell because it is the final closed-door meeting.

Paul is in effect telling the readers in the Corinthian church that there is always an exit, no matter what the trial. The same God who is faithful, the God who allowed the trial and who will not push you to the breaking point, will also provide a way out.

We may not always see the exit right away. Sometimes there are hardships so tangled that we fail to see any purpose, any real escape. Why does this child have to be ill? Why are thousands of people being killed in an ethnic war? Why does my country not respond to appeals for change? Why can I not find employment right now? Why does my relative hate me? Why is my own heart often so cold to the things that matter most? There are deep mysteries here. Yet God is faithful, and so there is an exit.

What kind of exit will we find? Sometimes it is healing. It may be peace, lasting peace in a war-torn country. Sometimes there is reconciliation. But at other times the exit is in waiting. There are lessons to learn that only hardship can teach.

The ultimate exit is death. This great enemy has become the exit by which we put off the "body of this death" (Romans 7:24 KJV) and enter into the consummate bliss of heaven. God has determined for each of us when is the best time for death, that passage taking us home. So, when we pray the Lord's Prayer and come to the petition, "Lead us not into temptation [trial], but deliver us from evil," we may not be aware of the radical measure we are requesting. There is only one final exit worth taking. It is the way across the River Jordan into the Celestial City.

The way out, then, is the way in. The premise is the faithful God. The means is Jesus Christ—the way, the truth, and the life (John 14:6). Jesus went through the most unimaginable trial—death on the cross—and found the exit through his endurance. He is, then, the "spiritual rock" that accompanies the children of God through their desert experience (1 Corinthians 10:4). For just as, by the rod of Moses, God had judged the physical rock on which he stood in the desert, so he judged his only Son by the rod of his own justice at Calvary. And just as water came pouring out of the rock in the desert (Exodus 17:6), so the water of life pours out of Jesus' deep well for all to live by (John 4:14).

This is life that no religion can offer. Neither the Taoist temple nor the higher Manichaean ethic will give such strength, such meaning. Only what Jesus did overcomes death itself and ushers in true freedom, the freedom of forgiveness and of power over all evil. This is real freedom. Freedom to exit, yes, but more than that, freedom to enter the fellowship of God. Of God's love for Alypius, Augustine could say, "You stretched out your almighty, ever merciful hand, O God, and rescued him from this madness. You taught him to trust in you, not in himself" (6.8). There is no greater good.

The spiritual says it best:

> I want Jesus to walk with me,
> I want Jesus to walk with me,
> all along my pilgrim journey, Lord,
> I want Jesus to walk with me.

> In my trials, Lord, walk with me,
> in my trials, Lord, walk with me,
> when the shades of life are falling, Lord,
> I want Jesus to walk with me.

> In my sorrows, Lord, walk with me,
> in my sorrows, Lord, walk with me,
> when my heart within is aching, Lord,
> I want Jesus to walk with me.

God's intention for us is even greater than going through trials and finding the way out. It is to find the way into his bosom. It is to know him and to be known by him. It is for Jesus to "walk with me" and commune with me forever.

The question of world religions has its answer here. There is an exit, which is at the same time the entrance to life. It is through Jesus Christ—the way, the truth, and the life. Does this mean there is no wisdom in the world religions, no partial truth? Certainly not. God generously pours out his gifts on women and men around the world. But none of them as a system, as a philosophy, presents God come down from heaven in order to suffer and die for his people. In none of them does God offer *himself* to his image-bearers as a friend for life. In none of them is grace upon grace showered in abundance on his beloved children. There are hardships, mysteries, unanswered questions. But one thing is sure:

> *God so loved the world that he gave his one and only Son, that whoever believes in him shall not perish but have eternal life. (John 3:16)*

Why not believe in him? You have nothing to lose that is worth keeping, and everything to gain you'd never want to lose.

NOTES

Chapter 2: The Real World

1. Quoted in Quentin J. Schultze, *Dancing in the Dark* (Grand Rapids: Eerdmans, 1991), 192.
2. Quoted in John Rewald, *The History of Impressionism* 4th ed. (London: Secker & Warburg, 1973), 431.

Chapter 3: Lifting the Veil

1. John Murray, *Redemption Accomplished and Applied* (Guildford: Banner of Truth, 1961), 107.

Chapter 4: You Are the Christ

1. Reported by Frederick Douglas, from *My Bondage and My Freedom*, 1855, quoted in Eileen Southern, *Readings in Black American Music* (New York: Norton, 1971), 83.
2. John Murray, *Redemption Accomplished and Applied*, 109.

Chapter 5: The Premise of Truth

1. Louis Berkhof, *Introduction to Systematic Theology* (Grand Rapids: Baker, 1979), 142–43.
2. Francis Turretin, *The Doctrine of Scripture*, trans. and ed. John W. Beardslee (Grand Rapids: Baker, 1981), 186.

Chapter 6: Collision Course

1. Philippus Lansbergen, *Bedenckingen op den dagelijckschen ende Iaerlijckschen loop van den Aardkloot* (Middelburg, 1629), 17.

Chapter 7: Science on Trial

1. Clarence Darrow to H. L. Mencken, 15 August, 1925, in *H. L. Mencken Collection*, New York Public Library, New York City. Quoted in Edward J. Larson, *Summer for the Gods: The Scopes Trial and America's Continuing Debate over Science and Religion* (New York: Basic Books, 1997), 190.
2. Charles Darwin, *The Origin of Species* (New York: Modern Library, 1948), 186–87.

Chapter 8: A Cloak of Decency

1. *Harper's Magazine*, special issue, summer 2000, 89–96.

Chapter 9: God and Evil

1. These thoughts are inspired by an article from Benjamin B. Warfield, "The Emotional Life of Our Lord," from *The Person and Work of Christ*, ed. Samuel G. Craig (Philadelphia: Presbyterian and Reformed, 1950), 93–145.
2. Ibid., 116–17.

INDEX OF PERSONS